China
since Mao

China
since Mao

Edited by Kwan Ha Yim

China
since Mao

First published in the USA 1980
First published in the UK 1980

Published by
THE MACMILLAN PRESS LTD
London and Basingstoke
Associated companies in Delhi
Dublin Hong Kong Johannesburg Lagos
Melbourne New York Singapore Tokyo

Printed in the United States of America
by Kingsport Press, Kingsport, Tenn.

British Library Cataloguing in Publication Data

China since Mao

   1. China—History—1976   I. Yim, Kwan Ha.
951.05   DS779.2
ISBN 0–333–28589–1

Contents

Introduction

MAO TSE-TUNG, WHO HAD DOMINATED Chinese politics for nearly three decades, passed away September 9, 1976, leaving behind him a China caught up in the contradiction between its commitment to permanent revolution and its intense desire for modernization. There were many uncertainties surrounding the make-up of the new political leadership, now bereft of the "helmsman," and about the direction in which the new leadership would steer the ship of state. At stake was not only the future of some 900 million people in the world's most populous nation, but also the balance of power on which rested the peace of the world. Former U.S. Secretary of State Henry A. Kissinger, who called Mao "one of the titans of our times," expressed the feeling of uncertainty: "I don't think any of us knows what the the new Chinese leaders will do." But more to the point, no one, whether inside or outside China, could predict *who* the new Chinese leaders would be. The world figuratively held its breath as the Chinese themselves sorted things out in the ensuing years through their political processes.

This volume represents an attempt to portray the course of events in post-Mao China from the death of Chou En-lai to the consolidation of a new regime under the du-umvirate of Chairman Hua Kuo-feng and Deputy Premier Teng Hsiao-ping. The period covered here, from January 1976 on through 1979, represents a transition period, which by definition was fluid. Events did not unfold according to any pre-determined line. There were unexpected twists and turns. If they seem, in retrospect, to fall into a pattern, it may be due to the power of hindsight with which historians are richly endowed.

Yet, one thing has emerged quite clearly: the post-Mao leadership has been able to redirect the nation's massive energies toward building a more modern and more productive society—away from the sterile preoccupation with ideological purity that had characterized Chinese politics during the last years of Mao's rule. The fall of "the Gang of Four" was the most spectacular manifestation of the new trend. Less dramatically, the change of direction affected the masses throughout the country. The new regime did not aspire to anything so

1

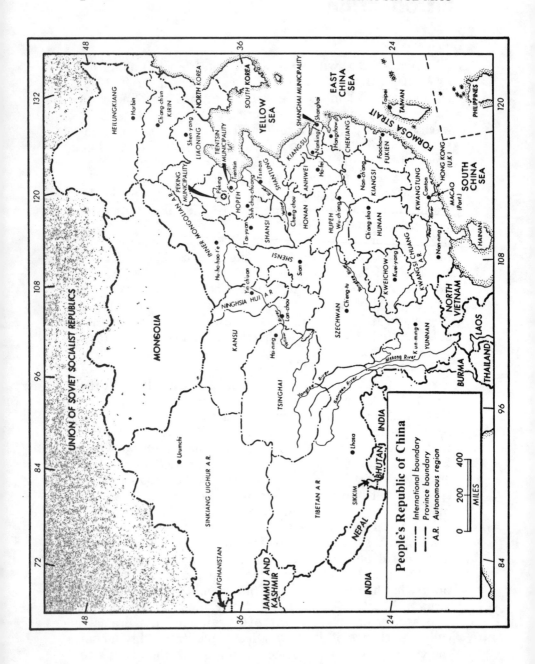

People's Republic of China

- - - - - International boundary
- - - - - Province boundary
A.R. Autonomous region

0   200   400
MILES

drastic as the complete restructuring of the Maoist political system or revision of the Maoist political ideology. What it attempted, within the framework of the inherited system, was a systematic campaign to reorient the entire nation toward new goals, to new modes of operation, to new ways of thinking. In the process, the god-like stature of Chairman Mao has been shed of its mystical glow.

That Mao Tse-tung was a great man will not be contested except by the most inveterate of his political foes. His conversion to Marxism-Leninism notwithstanding, Mao came perhaps the closest of all modern Chinese to the model of the peasant-emperor celebrated in Chinese historical lore: one who rises from rice paddies to the dragon throne at the outset of a new dynasty. Mao established his commanding presence at the apex of a totalitarian society he had helped to create. He ensconced himself behind the walls of Peking's Forbidden City, once the abode of the Manchu royal family. Although his simple life in his sparsely furnished study suggested nothing of imperial pomp, no one in his presence was spared the sense of overwhelming power emanating from his person. His oracular pronouncements settled matters. Even his casual remarks were listened to with deference. To the end of his life he kept his power jealously guarded against all pretenders.

Nonetheless, Mao was not wholly unaffected by human foibles brought on by old age and failing health. In the twilight of his life he brooded darkly over the imaginary conspiracy by "capitalist roaders" who he suspected were trying to undo all that had been accomplished for socialist reform. These "capitalist roaders" were his comrades, most of whom he had worked closely with through four decades of struggles with the Kuomintang, with the Japanese and finally with the Russians. He had them purged one by one. These included the venerable Liu Shao-chi, president of the People's Republic of China; Lin Piao, head of the People's Liberation Army and the one-time designated heir to the chairman; Teng Hsiao-ping, general secretary of the Chinese Communist Party; and Chen Po-ta, Mao's long-time secretary and confident. Premier Chou En-lai was one of the very few powerful men around Mao who somehow escaped the chairman's wrath. What saved him, apart from his administrative competence and loyalty to Mao, was probably the long illness, cancer, that confined him much of his last years to a hospital bed.

There may be a simpler psychological explanation for Mao's estrangement from his long-time friends and colleagues. That, however, is beside the point. For personal quarrels among public figures remain but rarely private. They tend to involve the public by being transformed into political issues. The more prominent the public figures, the greater the potential impact of their personal differences on politics. Mao's piques against his comrades took on a cosmic significance, engulfing the entire nation in a prolonged turmoil. Between 1966 and 1969 the world witnessed a bizarre spectacle of an aging revolutionary turning angry masses on his own party and state officials—in the name of "the Great Proletarian Cultural Revolution." Bands of youth, styling themselves as "Red Guards," roamed about the countryside in search of revolutionary experience. They attacked the "bourgeoisie," i.e. well-to-do Communist officials, managers and intellectuals. Afterwards, a new target was chosen; it turned out to be Confucius, who of course had been dead for many centuries.

As a political movement, the Cultural Revolution revolved around the clash of perspectives between ideologues and pragmatistic managers. But the ideologue-pragmatist dichotomy, if too tightly drawn, distorts the picture. Revolutionaries are ideologues by definition. They have to be pragmatic when they are put in charge of a state or even to survive in the rough and tumble of revolutionary politics. Mao's was a case in point. His principal contribution to the Chinese Revolution consisted in his theoretical writings interpreting Marxism-Leninism in the light of China's historical experiences. "Mao Tse-tung's Thought" laid down the ideological basis of the internal and external policies of the People's Republic of China. In that sense, Mao was an ideologue *par excellence*. At the same time, he distinguished himself as a political and military strategist. He appreciated the power of ideology and knew as well its limitations; he took care not to be misled by an "empty cannon" of political rhetoric.

Mao's forte as a political leader was mass mobilization. He excelled in striking a prophetic posture to summon his nation to great heights of selfless devotion. This particular forte served him and his party well in the early phase of the Revolution, when the task at hand was getting people to change their old ways and embrace the new order. Its usefulness became more questionable as the new regime settled down to the business of governing a nation. His estrangement from his colleagues came shortly after the failure of the "Great Leap Forward" in 1958. It was an ambitious project that was to transform China into a Communist state in one great leap. Launched with more gusto than realism, hasty collectivization of farms and backyard furnaces wreaked havoc with China's fledging industrialization. Mao had to admit his mistakes. In 1959 he resigned his presidency, retaining the largely honorific position of chairman of the Chinese Communist Party (CCP). (He complained that he was being treated like a dead ancestor.) It was not until the Cultural Revolution moved into full swing that the "Great Helmsman" recovered his position in the direction of Chinese affairs.

The Cultural Revolution also brought Chiang Ching, the Chairman's wife, to a position of prominence and power. A former Shanghai actress, Chiang Ching had entered the tightly knit circle of the CCP's elite at Yenan, the CCP's wartime capital, through her marriage to Chairman Mao. She had not been through the Long March, which meant that she did not have standing in her own right in the status-conscious CCP hierarchy. The Cultural Revolution was to be her Long March. She formed an alliance with Mao's protegé and Minister of Defense, Lin Piao, and surrounded herself with a coterie of Shanghai-based radical firebrands: Chang Chun-chiao, Wang Hung-wen and Yao Wen-yuan.

Chiang Ching's proximity to Mao, coupled with the support of the PLA (People's Liberation Army), gave her and her friends a well-nigh unassailable position. She spoke in the name of the revered Chairman, calling on the masses to rebel. And the youth by the millions responded. It was an awesome display of power. It caught the party and state officials completely unprepared, as the assault on them was made in the name of "Mao Tse-tung's Thought," which they themselves believed in. They were driven out of office and publicly humiliated. In terms of smashing the power structure, the Cultural

Revolution succeeded beyond the wildest of expectations. Within three years Chiang Ching and two of her friends— Chang Chun-chiao and Yao Wen-yuan—made it to the CCP Politburo membership. In 1973, the youngest of the Shanghai Radicals, Wang Hung-wen, was elected Deputy Chairman of the CCP, ranking next to Chou En-lai. But their power was a reflection of Mao's; it did not last long after the Chairman's death. Thus, within a period of ten years, Chiang Ching and her friends had climbed to the summit of power only to experience a precipitous fall and to be relegated to at least immediate history as the infamous "Gang of Four."

A worse fate befell Lin Piao. A veteran of the Long March, Lin had been one of the most loyal followers of Mao's. It was he who delivered and maintained the PLA support for the Cultural Revolution. History may well record him as a victim of his success. As the political machinery of the party and state crumbled all over the country under the attack of the Red Guards, the PLA emerged as the only organized force capable of restoring public order. The army not only moved in to fill the political vacuum; it played a key role in reconstructing the party and state apparatus at the local level. This brought Lin Piao an enormous political leverage. At the Ninth Party Congress, which was convened in April 1969, Lin was named the sole Vice Chairman of the party, Mao's "closest comrade in arms" and successor. In retrospect, this turned out to be the beginning of his end. Neither Mao nor Chou En-lai appeared to feel comfortable with the prospect of the simple-minded Lin leading the country after their time. They set into motion characteristically deft maneuvers that drove a wedge between Lin Piao and the Cultural Revolution group and set other army leaders against Lin. Outmaneuvered, Lin apparently contemplated a military coup against Mao in the summer of 1971. The coup was aborted. He is said to have fled the country in a British-built Trident jet plane that crashed in Mongolia the night of September 12-13.

The post-Cultural Revolution policy of the People's Republic of China, especially after the fall of Lin Piao, presaged a post-Mao reorientation. The important decisions regarding the normalization of diplomatic relations with the United

States and China's modernization were taken in this period by Mao Tse-tung and Chou En-lai. These decisions set the framework for the policies that their succesors have since pursued. That this framework has held thus far, in spite of political turmoil, testifies to the statesman-like courage and foresight of the two great revolutionaries.

On the other hand, post-Mao China has found that while it could live with Mao's policy, it could not with his politics. As his end approached—he was eighty-two years old when he died—Mao was concerned about the future of his wife and her radical friends. He had Chou En-lai put together a shaky coalition of moderate bureaucrats and the Cultural Revolution Left. Mao's personal choice of Hua Kuo-feng to succeed Chou En-lai, when the latter died in January 1976, was quite probably intended to continue the coalition policy. But the coalition did not survive Mao's death. Mao's policies were to be carried out by those who had been the victims of his purges.

The factual material in this book is drawn largely from the record compiled by FACTS ON FILE in its weekly coverage of world history.

KWAN HA YIM

Valley Cottage, N.Y.
March, 1980

The End of an Era: 1976

Chou En-lai Dies

In human terms the year 1976 marks a great divide in the history of the People's Republic of China (PRC). Three of its most senior leaders died in succession that year: Chou En-lai, premier of the PRC since its founding in 1949; Chu Te, one of the founders of the People's Liberation Army and chairman of the National People's Congress; and finally, Mao Tse-tung.

The year opened with the news that Premier Chou had died of cancer Jan. 8 in Peking. He was 78 years old. The announcement of Chou's death was made Jan. 9 by Hsinhua, the official Chinese news agancy. It was issued in the name of the major governing bodies of China, including the Communist Party, the National People's Congress and the State Council. It extolled Chou as "a great proletarian revolutionary of the Chinese people, a loyal revolutionary fighter of the Chinese people and an outstanding, long-tested leader of the party and the state." After Chou fell ill in 1972, the notice added, "meticulous" attempts to treat him had been made by medical personnel "under the constant and affectionate attention of our great leader, Chairman Mao, and the party's Central Committee."

Chou En-lai was born in 1899, the son of well-to-do gentry in Chekiang Province. He went to study in France and Japan and belonged to that generation of the Chinese who turned to communism for an answer to the problem of ridding China of the twin evils of foreign domination and warlordism.

In the mid-1920s, Chou En-lai worked as the head of the Political Department of the Whampoa Military Academy at Canton, the superintendent of which was Chiang Kai-shek. The Chinese Communists were then collaborating with the Nationalists, the Kuomintang, in a united front directed against the warlords. When the united front broke down in 1927, Chou went underground with other Chinese Communist leaders. With their urban bases destroyed, the Communists moved to rural areas. This period, known as the Kiangsi Soviet period (1931-34), marked the beginning of cooperation between Chou En-lai and Mao Tse-tung, who became an increasingly strong force in the Communist movement.

9

Chou participated in the "Long March" of 1934-35, the legendary trek of 6,000 miles through mountain paths and marshlands while pursued by the Kuomintang forces. He continued to play a key role in the CCP (Chinese Communist Party) through the decades of the civil war, Japanese aggression and the establishment of the People's Republic.

In the aftermath of the Cultural Revolution of 1966-69, he engineered the restoration of the party and state apparatus. He put together and presided over a shaky coalition between two factions: the Cultural Revolution Left (Radicals), formed around Chiang Ching, Chairman Mao's wife, and the civil and military officials (moderates) represented by Deputy Premier Teng Hsiao-ping. Teng had been purged during the Cultural Revolution as a "capitalist roader," but he was reinstated in 1973 by Premier Chou.

The coalition between the two groups became precarious after the premier's death. A wall poster, reminiscent of one during the Cultural Revolution, made its appearance at Peking University Feb. 10, attacking the political attitudes and policies of Deputy Premier Teng. Although the poster did not mention Teng by name, it quoted one of his most controversial statements to the effect that "I do not care whether a cat is black or white, the important thing is whether it catches mice." Uttered during the period of economic retrenchment in the aftermath of the Great Leap Forward (1958-59), it suggested Teng's pragmatic, moderate approach to politics.

The attacks on Teng ran 43 pages in the poster, alluding to "a capitalist roader who formed cliques around himself and denigrated ideology in favor of economic progress." The wall poster campaign against Teng spread Feb. 12-21 to the universities, factories and streets of the cities of Shanghai, Wuhan and Hangchow and the province of Liaoning.

A front-page article in *Jenmin Jih Pao* (*People's Daily*) Feb. 17 charged unnamed "capitalist roaders" in the party with attempting to dilute Chairman Mao Tse-tung's call for "class struggle." They stressed, the article charged, the study of the "dictatorship of the proletariat," which was linked to the more meliorist goals of economic progress and social stability. The article also accused the Teng faction of having split the party.

The polarity was allegedly brought on through the appointment of "unreformed bourgeois intellectuals" to committee ranks.

Wall posters at Peking's Tsinghua University Feb. 19-20 quoted 100 examples of allegedly anti-Mao remarks made by Teng, and students at Peking University Feb. 28 demanded that Teng be purged from the government. *Jenmin Jih Pao* Feb. 28 gave an indication that Teng was clinging to his position of power. The party newspaper, though not identifying him by name, said that Teng was "persevering in the revisionist line of Liu Shao-chi and Lin Piao."

The political campaign directed against Teng and alleged "unrepentant capitalist roaders" in the Communist Party climaxed April 7 with the government announcement that Teng had been deposed and Acting Premier Hua Kuo-feng elevated to the second-ranked position after Communist Party Chairman Mao. The government action followed a day of rioting April 5 in Peking by presumed supporters of the late Premier Chou En-lai. The outbursts were linked to Teng.

Word of Teng's ouster came in a text released April 7 by Hsinhua, the official press agency. It said that Teng had been dismissed from "all posts both inside and outside the party," including those of deputy party chairman, first deputy premier and chief of staff of the armed forces. Teng was allowed to retain his party membership "so as to see how he will behave himself in the future," an apparent reference to political recantation.

Simultaneously, Hsinhua announced that Hua Kuo-feng, who had been chosen above Teng to succeed the late Premier Chou, had been designated premier and first deputy chairman of the Communist Party.

Teng's ouster signified a momentary surge of power for the Shanghai-based radicals around Chiang Ching, who had seized control of the party's propaganda apparatus, the secret police and mass organizations. They were young, energetic and vocal, but they were ranged against older and more experienced groups of civil and military officials. The newly appointed Premier Hua continued essentially Chou's policy of mediating between the two power groups.

To project a facade of unity, the Peking leadership took care to seat "radicals" and "moderates" side by side at the May Day celebration, which was seen on national television. Analysts quoted in the *New York Times* May 2 said that this was the first such public expression of unity since the purge of Teng. The purge had increased tension between the two ideological camps. Prominent leftists at the function included Chiang Ching and Yao Wen-yuan, a Politburo member from Shanghai. Hua Kuo-feng, who was considered a relative moderate, presided over the occasion. Also present were Deputy Premier Li Hsien-nien and Defense Minister Yeh Chien-ying, both regarded as moderates.

Nonetheless, the Cultural Revolution Left kept up the barrage of ideological attacks on the moderates, using Teng as their target. An article appeared in *Jenim Jih Pao* May 7 to commemorate the 10th anniversary of Mao Tse-tung's promulgation of the "May 7th Directive." It pointed out that the essence of Mao's directive was the criticism of "revisionism and the bourgeoisie." Mao was quoted as having said: "You are making the socialist revolution, and yet don't know where the bourgeoisie is. It is right in the Communist Party—those in power taking the capitalist road."

The article criticized Teng as the "behind-the-scenes promoter of the bourgeoisie inside and outside of the party." It urged that all exponents of "bourgeois rights" be criticized and Mao's directives be studied as a guideline to such criticism.

A second article, prepared jointly by *Jenmin Jih Pao, Chiehfang Chun Pao* (*Liberation Army Daily*) and *Hung Chi* (*Red Flag*), the party's theoretical journal, appeared as an editorial May 16 in commemoration of the May 16, 1966 "Circular of the Central Committee of the Communist Party," another important anti-rightist document of the cultural revolution. The article warned against the restoration of capitalism by "capitalist roaders." This group, the article said, continued to hold "a very large portion of party and state power."

Earthquakes Strike Northern China

In July 1976, the Chinese people mourned the death of another first generation revolutionary, Chu Te. Chu, the grand old man of the People's Liberation Army and chairman of the National People's Congress, died July 6 at the age of 90. Chu's death, coming after Chou's, left Mao Tse-tung as the last of the trio to survive. But Mao, aged 82, was himself reported in failing health, pointing to a generational change that was in progress in Peking.

In ancient China belief persisted that natural calamities accompanied the end of a dynastic cycle. A modern version of the traditional pattern was seen in two great earthquakes that struck heavily populated areas of northern China July 28. The first shock, which occurred at about 3:40 a.m. July 28, registered 8.2 on the Richter earthquake scale at the U.S. Geological Survey facility in Golden, Colo., making it the strongest quake registered since the March 28, 1964 earthquake in Alaska. The second tremor, which struck 16 hours later, about 67 miles north of Tangshan and 60 miles east of Peking, registered 7.9 on the Richter scale.

Apparently, these earthquakes had been anticipated. During a June visit of American earthquake specialists, Chinese experts had predicted that magnetic changes in the Tientsin area presaged a major earthquake before the 1980s. Radio stations in Peking and Tientsin had warned the populace throughout 1975 to prepare for a quake; there was, however, no evidence that an evacuation order had been given. Such an order was given on the eve of a devastating tremor that shook China's Liaoning Peninsula Feb. 4, 1975 and was thought to have saved thousands of lives.

The American scientific group, led by Dr. C. Barry Raleigh of the U.S. Geological Survey Center in Menlo Park, Calif., had gone to China in June to meet with Chinese earthquake specialists. Interviewed by the *New York Times* July 29, Raleigh said his group had been told that a study of major earthquakes over the past few centuries indicated an ominous pattern of earthquake migration toward northeast China.

In Peking, casualties and damage were reported to be light, although many buildings suffered extensive damage, and rubble littered many streets. Heavy casualties and damages occurred in and around the mining and industrial city of Tangshan, which was at or near the epicenter of the first quake, about 105 miles southeast of Peking. According to Western news dispatches from Peking July 31, about 100,000 persons were believed killed. The *Washington Post* reported Aug. 1 that, according to the Bulgarian news agency, Dobri Donchev, the Bulgarian envoy to Peking, was told by a high Chinese official that one million persons may have been killed or injured. The Chinese government did not release the exact casualty figures. Foreign estimates ranged from 100,000 to one million.

The Chinese government immediately undertook a massive relief work for the disaster-stricken areas. Trucks, troop convoys, mobile field hospitals and amphibious vehicles were sent into Tangshan. The U.S. Liaison Office in Peking offered "any assistance that might be wanted." Hsinhua, the official Chinese press agency, reported that Premier Hua Kuo-feng July 30 had toured the mining and industrial city, visiting the Kailan coal mines and the Tangshan iron and steel plant. Hua expressed sympathy to the victims and urged them to restore industrial production and rebuild their homes.

The relief effort numbered 56 medical teams, 800 medical workers and divisions of both the People's Liberation Army and the civilian-staffed People's Militia. Their work was hampered by 15 new aftershocks measuring 5 or higher on the open-ended Richter scale. Some of the relief workers were killed in the aftershocks, *Jenmin Jih Pao* said Aug. 2.

Officials said in radio broadcasts Aug. 2 that "an overwhelming majority" of the workers in the Kailan mines when the quake struck had been able to return to the surface safely. No mention was made, however, of the rest of Tangshan's population, which was thought to be in bed when the quake struck shortly before dawn.

Officials of the Chinese government warned July 29 and 30 that new shocks might occur closer to Peking. The capital's residents were urged to remain out of doors, and most did so in spite of torrential downpours. They erected tents, lean-tos and other makeshift shelters. Many remained in their outdoor shelters through July 31.

Most foreigners at first were slow to heed the advice but complied when the high-rise buildings in which they were staying shook violently during the second tremor. Most headed for their embassies or for tents that had been set up on the tennis courts of the Chinese-run recreation club for foreigners. Foreigners were barred from Tangshan after the shock, and those in the city were flown to Peking. In warning foreign embassies of the probability of further quakes, Chinese officials said "abnormal things are happening in the Tientsin-Tangshan area, and people should take precautions." The abnormalities were believed to include erratic behavior among animals and changes in well water, frequently cited harbingers of earthquakes.

Foreign embassy staff members and families began leaving Peking Aug. 1 after Chinese officials warned embassies of continuing post-quake tremors in Tangshan. The officials also warned that the epicenter of the new disturbances appeared to be moving steadily toward Peking. Many businessmen also left Peking for Hong Kong or Tokyo. David Dean, deputy chief of the American liaison office in Peking, said Aug. 1 that 19 U.S. dependents had left on flights to Tokyo and that the remaining 11 staff members would be brought out later.

Fifty British dependents and 25 Australians also left on special planes to Canton in South China, Reuters reported Aug. 1. Chinese officials assisted in the evacuation of 15 Egyptians and the entire Lebanese embassy staff, as well as those of some African countries. The French embassy staffers remained in Peking, according to Reuters.

The Peking railroad station was closed Aug. 2, and Peking's six million residents remained, for the most part, camped in the streets, awaiting further official instructions. Although there had been no reports of epidemics, foreigners arriving in Hong Kong told of poor hygienic conditions. One case of meningitis was reported Aug. 3 by the London *Times*.

Six new aftershocks Aug. 8 and 9 struck the Tangshan-Peking region, prompting officials Aug. 10 to repeat their warning that another serious earthquake was imminent and that Peking residents should remain out of doors. Most of the aftershocks occurred near the original quake epicenter of Tangshan, although a brief tremor measuring from 4 to 5 on the Richter scale was said to have hit Peking Aug. 9, the news agency Reuters reported. Most of the Tangshan shocks measured between 5 and 6 on the scale, and the two strongest measured 6 and 6.2, the Chinese Foreign Ministry said Aug. 10.

The warning followed almost a week of calm that had led many Peking residents to return temporarily to their homes. Most had gone only to wash or sleep for the night or to take refuge from torrential rains. No signs were seen of the outdoor shelters being torn down. The Peking Hotel, which had been expected to reopen Aug. 9, remained closed as a result of the warning, and access to the two other towers housing foreigners remained limited.

Production resumed at one pit in the Kailan coal mines near Tangshan, Radio Peking reported Aug. 8. Other reports Aug. 11 referred to workers "determined to build a new Tangshan iron and steel company." This implied that the Tangshan steel foundries had been destroyed. In addition, foreign sources said that Chinese officials had told them that a hospital and a train bound for Peking had been buried almost completely during the original quake July 28, Reuters reported Aug. 8. The same foreign sources also said they had been told that 40,000 refugees from Tangshan had been moved into central China.

A strong new earthquake hit the southwestern province of Szechuan Aug. 16 but inflicted only slight damage, according to Hsinhua. Although the agency did not cite casualty or damage figures, it said that the degree of damage was "very slight because the Chinese seismological department had forecast the earthquake and the Szechuan provincial party committee had taken precautionary measures beforehand."

This explanation was confirmed by foreigners working in the area, who told the Toronto *Globe and Mail* Aug. 17 that evacuation warnings had been issued before the quake. Another explanation given for the low degree of damage inflicted by the quake, which registered 7.2 on the Richter scale, was the sparse population of the area hit by the quake. Sungpan and Pingwu, the towns closest to the quake's epicenter, were mining towns of fewer than 20,000 inhabitants each. The new quake followed the lifting Aug. 15 of the tremor alert in Peking. The alert had been in force for 16 days.

Meanwhile, Peking citizens began demolishing badly damaged buildings and repairing structures that were judged safe in the wake of the July 28 earthquake, the *Globe and Mail* reported Aug. 13. Among the buildings reported to be unsafe and ready for demolition were the Capital House, a hospital built and equipped by the Rockefeller Foundation before 1949, and the residential quarters for foreign students of the Languages Institute and Peking University.

The Death of Chairman Mao

While the Chinese were recovering from the shocks of the earthquakes they received the news of another event of comparable impact: Chairman Mao died Sept. 9, 1976 in Peking at the age of 82.

The announcement of Mao's death came over Radio Peking at 4 p.m. Peking time, 16 hours after he died at 12:10 a.m. The message said that Mao died "because of the worsening of his illness and despite all treatment, although meticulous medical care was given him in every way after he fell ill." The announcement was made by Hsinhua, the official Chinese news agency, on behalf of the party's central committee, the central committee's military commission, the state council of the People's Republic and the standing committee of the National People's Congress. The announcement included an appeal to the people to "continue to carry out Chairman Mao's revolutionary line and policies in foreign affairs resolutely."

The message also urged the country to "deepen the criticism" of former Deputy Premier Teng Hsiao-ping, who had fallen from power in the political struggle that followed Premier Chou En-lai's death in January. The broadcast asked the Chinese to "uphold the unity and unification of the party and closely rally round the party central committee." The message did not name any possible successor to Mao.

The cause of Mao's death remained unclear, although the *Washington Post* reported Sept. 10 that Chinese officials had told one foreign visitor that Mao had suffered a stroke recently. In addition, the *New York Times* Sept. 10 quoted a Viennese doctor as saying he had been told that Mao had suffered from Parkinson's disease. Mao's last public appearance had been May 1, 1971 when he viewed a fireworks display in Peking.

The last foreign official to meet with Mao was Pakistani Premier Zulfikar Ali Bhutto May 27. Bhutto said after that meeting that he thought Mao had a cold. A telecast of their talks in Peking showed Mao stooped and apparently weak.

Outpourings of popular grief were reported throughout China Sept. 9. "The Internationale," the Socialist anthem, was played throughout Peking as 2,000 persons gathered in Tien An Men Square. Some wept openly; many wore black armbands or white mourning flowers. Front pages of Sept. 10 newspapers displayed full-page photographs of Mao bordered in black. Reports from the countryside outside Peking cited immediate work stoppages and funeral processions after the announcement. Within minutes of the broadcast, which was replayed throughout the night of Sept. 9, peasants had put on black armbands.

Officials immediately scheduled eight days of memorial ceremonies, beginning Sept. 11 and ending Sept. 18. For the last day of mourning a televised memorial rally was scheduled for Tien An Men Square. Until that date, Mao's body lay in state in the Great Hall of the People, and flags flew at half-staff. The announcement of Mao's death said that no foreign leaders would be invited to Peking during the period of mourning.

Official Responses from Abroad

Many world leaders voiced their regret at Mao's death. U.S. President Ford said that Mao had moved "to end a generation of hostility and to launch a new and more positive era of relations" between the U.S. and China. Ford called Mao a "most remarkable and very great man." Former U.S. President Richard M. Nixon, who had met Mao twice, called him "a unique man in a generation of great revolutionary leaders" and praised his "immense physical courage and ideological determination."

Japan reacted strongly to Mao's death. Premier Takeo Miki Sept. 9 expressed his "deep grief" in a personal call to the Chinese embassy in Tokyo. Newspapers in Japan had black-bordered headlines reading "Mao's gone," and television stations broadcast biographies of the Chinese leader throughout the evening.

French President Valery Giscard d'Estaing said that the death of Mao "extinguished a beacon of world thought."

Pakistani Premier Zulfikar Ali Bhutto, who was the last foreign statesman to see Mao, called Mao "the son of revolution, its very essence, indeed, its rhythm and romance, the supreme architect of a brilliant new order shaking the world." "Men like Mao come once in a century," Bhutto added.

Indian Prime Minister Indira Gandhi, whose government had been seeking to normalize relations with China, said that Mao was "an eminent statesman who led the resurgence and progress of the Chinese people."

In Taiwan, Mao's death was celebrated with firecrackers, cheers and predictions that the demise of Communist rule in China had begun, the *Washington Post* reported Sept. 10. Radio broadcasts reviled Mao as a "bandit leader" and "the greatest criminal in Chinese history."

Cuba, which had criticized China and Mao in the months before his death, had no immediate comment. Nor did Eastern European Communist countries. The Soviet Union, whose relations with China during the last 10½ years of Mao's rule had been marked by a bitter political and doctrinal rivalry, made no public comment. The central committee of the Soviet Communist Party, however, sent a brief telegram of "deep condolences," adding "sympathy for the family and relatives of the deceased." The move was seen by experts as a conciliatory gesture toward China's new leaders that was aimed at healing the rupture in Sino-Soviet relations.

China's probable future orientation toward Moscow and Washington was not then clear, although the announcement of Mao's death suggested few changes in foreign policy. "We must...unite with all the forces in the world that can be knitted, and carry the struggle against imperialism, social-imperialism and modern revisionism to the end," the radio broadcast said. "Social-imperialism" and "modern revisionism" were commonly-used Chinese expressions to designate Soviet attempts to dominate world socialism.

U.S. Secretary of State Henry A. Kissinger, calling Mao "one of the titans of our times," said that he was uncertain of the future of U.S.-Chinese relations. "I don't think any of us knows what the new Chinese leaders will do," he said.

The Mourning for Mao

The official observance of the mourning for Mao began Sept. 11. The first ceremony was a private series of services Sept. 12 for party and army officials at the Great Hall of the People, where Chiang Ching, Mao's widow, laid a wreath bearing the names of Mao's surviving family. The ceremony began the open display of Mao's body in the Great Hall.

During the eight-day mourning period, more than 300,000 persons viewed the body, and Chinese workers made a number of sacrifices in Mao's memory. As a tribute to Mao, most factory and agricultural workers went to work on what would have been their day off on Sunday, Sept. 12. All recreational facilities and stores selling nonessential goods were closed during the mourning period. Nearly all Peking residents wore both black armbands and white flowers to signify their grief.

Foreigners were able to view Mao's body Sept. 13. Albanians, whose "antirevisionist" ideology was termed closest to that of Mao, filed past the glass-enclosed body first. North Koreans, Vietnamese and Cambodians followed, with each country's delegation leader laying a wreath next to the glass catafalque. James R. Schlesinger, former U.S. secretary of defense, and his family, who had been in China at Mao's invitation, also viewed the body. (Schlesinger continued his China tour Sept. 14, when he went to Kweilin. He also visited Tibet, Sinkiang and Inner Mongolia, areas that normally were off-limits to foreigners.)

The eight days of mourning ended Sept. 18 with a brief rally of an estimated one million people in Tien An Men Square. The rally followed a three-minute period of silence during which Chinese stopped working and paid silent tribute to Mao. During the rally, Premier Hua Kuo-feng gave a memorial speech in which he called on the army, the party and the people of China to "carry on the cause left behind by Chairman Mao." Hua reviewed Mao's revolutionary career, his struggles with a long line of "opportunists," and his achievements in raising China's status to that of an independent power. Hua also called for ideological continuity and unity and greater criticism of purged former premier Teng Hsiao-ping.

After the speech, the mourners, comprising party and military delegations from all over China, bowed three times to a portrait of Mao over the podium. Then "The East is Red," the anthem of Chinese communism, was played, and many mourners wept.

An air of uncertainty hung over Peking. It was not clear who would succeed to the mantle of Chairman Mao. The official list of the committee for Mao's funeral, published Sept. 10, established a tentative hierarchy of high Chinese officials. Leaders, in the order that they appeared on the list, were: Hua Kuo-feng, first vice party chairman and premier; Wang Hung-wen, party vice chairman; Yeh Chien-ying, party vice chairman and defense premier; Chiang Ching. Mao's widow; Chang Chun-chiao, vice premier; Yao Wen-yuan, Shanghai official and leading polemicist; Li Hsien-nien, vice premier and finance expert; Chen Hsi-lien, Peking region military commander; Chi Teng-kuei, first political commissar of the Peking military region; Wang Tung-hsing, director of the Central Committee general office and former Mao bodyguard; Wu Teh, mayor of Peking; Hsu Shih-yu, Canton military region commander; Wei Kuo-ching, Kwangtung provincial revolutionary committee chairman; Li Te-sheng, Shenyang military region commander; and Chen Yung-kuei, vice chairman of the Shansi provincial revolutionary committee and hero of the Tachai production brigade.

Omitted from the list were Chou Jung-hsin, minister of education; Wan Li, minister of railways, and Chu Mu-chih, director of Hsinhua, the official press agency, the *New York Times* noted Sept. 11. They were thought to have been purged because of their ties to Teng Hsiao-ping, the *Times* said. Chou had been attacked in wall posters at Tsingha University in Peking in December 1975, while Wan may have been blamed for repeated worker railroad strife. Little was known about Chu.

Despite the uncertainty about China's top leadership, an editorial outlining future policy appeared Sept. 16 in *Jenmin Jih Pao*, the official party newspaper. The editorial, duplicated in both the ideological paper and the army paper, called for Chinese to "act according to the principles laid down" and "carry on the cause left by Chairman Mao."

Also unresolved at the end of the mourning period was the question of what to do with Mao's body. Officials recalled anger expressed in some quarters at the cremation of Chou En-lai's body following his death in January. It was not until Oct. 8 that Peking announced its decision that Mao's body would be embalmed and enshrined in a crystal sarcophagus and displayed in a mausoleum to be constructed in Peking. The decision was made, said the announcement, "so that the broad masses of the people would be able to pay respects to the remains."

Excerpts from Statement Announcing Mao's Death

These are excerpts from the Sept. 9 statement issued by Hsinhua, the Chinese news agency, and published in the *New York Times* Sept. 10, 1976:

"Comrade Mao Tse-tung, the esteemed and beloved great leader of our party, our army and the people of all nationalities of our country, the great teacher of the international proletariat and the oppressed nations and oppressed people, chairman of the central committee of the Communist Party of China, chairman of the military commission of the central committee of the Communist Party of China, and honorary chairman of the national committee of the Chinese People's Political Consultative Conference, passed away at 00:10 hours, Sept. 9, 1976, in Peking, because of the worsening of his illness and despite all treatment, although meticulous medical care was given him in every way after he fell ill.

"Chairman Mao Tse-tung was the founder and wise leader of the Communist Party of China, the Chinese People's Liberation Army and the People's Republic of China. Chairman Mao led our party in waging a protracted, acute and complex struggle against the right and left opportunist lines in the party, defeating the opportunist lines pursued by Chen Tu-hsiu. Chu Chiu-pai, Li Li-san, Lo Chang-lung, Wang Ming, Chang Kuotao, Kao Kang, Jao Shu-shih and Peng Teh-huai and again, during the great proletarian Cultural Revolution, triumphing over the counterrevolutionary revisionist line of Liu Shao-chi, Lin Piao and Teng Hsiao-ping, thus enabling our party to develop and grow in strength steadily in class struggle and the struggle between the two lines....

"During the period of the new democratic revolution, Chairman Mao, in accordance with the universal truth of Marxism-Leninism and by combining it with the concrete practice of the Chinese revolution, creatively laid down the general line and general policy of the new democratic revolution, founded the Chinese People's Liberation Army and pointed out that the seizure of political power by armed force in China could be achieved only by following the road of building rural base areas, using the countryside to encircle the cities and finally seizing the cities, and not by any other road...."

"The victory of the Chinese people's revolution led by Chairman Mao changed the situation in the East and the world and blazed a new trail for the cause of liberation of the oppressed nations and oppressed people.

"In the period of the socialist revolution, Chairman Mao comprehensively summed up the positive as well as the negative experience of the international Communist movement, penetratingly analyzed the class relations in socialist society and, for the first time in the history of the development of Marxism, unequivocally pointed out that there are still classes and class struggle after the Socialist transformation of the ownership of the means of production has in the main been completed, drew the scientific conclusion that the bourgeoisie is right in the Communist Party, put forth the great theory of continuing the revolution under the dictatorship of the proletariat, and laid down the party's basic line for the entire historical period of socialism.

"All the victories of the Chinese people were achieved under the leadership of Chairman Mao; they are all great victories for Mao Tse-tung thought.

"The radiance of Mao Tse-tung thought will forever illuminate the road to advance of the Chinese people....

"With the great boldness and vision of a proletarian revolutionary, he initiated in the international Communist movement the great struggle to criticize modern revisionism with the Soviet revisionist renegade clique at the core, promoted the vigorous development of the cause of the world proletarian revolution and the cause of all the people of all countries against imperialism and hegemonism, and pushed the history of mankind foreward. Chairman Mao Tse-tung was the greatest Marxist of the contemporary era....

"The central committee of the Communist Party of China calls on the whole party, the whole army and the people of all nationalities throughout the country to turn their grief into strength with determination:

"We must carry on the cause left behind by Chairman Mao and persist in taking class struggle as the key link, keep to the party's basic line and persevere in continuing the revolution under the dictatorship of the proletariat.

"We must carry on the cause left behind by Chairman Mao and strengthen the centralized leadership of the party, resolutely uphold the unity and unification of the party and closely rally round the party central committee.

"We must strengthen the building of the party ideologically and organizationally in the course of the struggle between the two lines and resolutely implement the principle of the three-in-one combination of the old, middle-aged and young in accordance with the five requirements for bringing up successors to the cause of the proletarian revolution.

"We must carry on the cause left behind by Chairman Mao and consolidate the great unity of the people of all nationalities under the leadership of the working class and based on the worker-peasant alliance, deepen the criticism of Teng Hsiaoping, continue the struggle to repulse the right deviationist attempt to reverse correct verdicts, consolidate and develop the victories of the great proletarian Cultural Revolution, enthusiastically support the new socialist things, restrict bourgeois right and further consolidate the dictatorship of the proletariat in our country.

"We should continue to unfold the three great revolutionary movements of class struggle, the struggle for production and scientific experiment, build our country independently and with the initiative in our own hands, through self-reliance, hard struggle, diligence and thrift, and go all out, aim high and acheive greater, faster, better and more economic results in building socialism.

"We must carry on the cause left behind by Chairman Mao and resolutely implement his line on army building, strengthen the building of the army, strengthen the building of the militia, strengthen preparedness against war, heighten our vigilance, and be ready at all times to wipe out any enemy that dares to intrude. We are determined to liberate Taiwan.

"We must carry on the cause left behind by Chairman Mao and continue to carry out Chairman Mao's revolutionary line and policies in foreign affairs resolutely.

"We must adhere to proletarian internationalism, strengthen the unity between our party and the genuine Marxist-Leninist parties and organizations all over the world, strengthen the unity between the people of our country and the people of all other countries, especially those of the third-world countries, unite with all the forces in the world that can be knitted, and carry the struggle against imperialism, social-imperialism and modern revisionism through to the end.

"We will never seek hegemony and will never be a super-power.

"We must carry on the cause left behind by Chairman Mao and assiduously study Marxism-Leninism-Mao Tse-tung thought, apply ourselves to the study of works by Marx, Engels, Lenin and Stalin and works by Chairman Mao, fight for the complete overthrow of the bourgeoisie and all other exploiting classes, for the establishment of the dictatorship of the proletariat in place of the dictatorship of the bourgeoisie and for the triumph of socialism over capitalism, and strive to build our country into a powerful socialist state, make a still greater contribution to humanity and realize the ultimate goal of communism.

"Long live invincible Marxism-Leninism-Mao Tse-tung thought!

"Long live the great, glorious and correct Communist Party of China!

"Eternal glory to our great leader and teacher Chairman Mao Tse-tung!"

The Defeat of the Radicals

The Succession Problem

With Mao Tse-tung now dead in September 1976, speculation as to who might succeed him centered around the following six persons:

■ Hua Kuo-feng, who had been named premier in April, was thought to be a logical compromise choice for both radicals and moderates.

■ Chang Chun-chiao, deputy premier and a former propagandist during the civil war, reportedly had detached himself from the two factions but had the support of many radicals. His experience as party secretary reportedly made him a candidate for Communist Party leadership.

■ Wang Hung-wen, a young radical in the Mao tradition, who held the post of deputy party chairman behind Mao, had the support of many radicals seeking younger leadership. Wang had risen to prominence during the Cultural Revolution and reportedly had been Mao's first choice to replace Chou as premier.

■ Yeh Chien-ying, minister of defense, was considered a moderate. At age 79, he was considered too old to replace Mao.

■ Chiang Ching, Mao's wife and another prominent radical, was thought to be too abrasive for a top party or government post; however, she was then believed to have considerable influence in the choice of Mao's eventual successor.

■ Li Hsien-nien, deputy premier for economic affairs, was one of the few moderates who remained in power after Chou's death and the purge of Teng Hsiao-ping, but he was not considered powerful enough to secure a top post.

Behind the facade of unity (the air was filled with fervent appeals to the memories of Chairman Mao) the struggle for succession intensified, with both the radicals and the moderates claiming their legitimacy in terms of Maoism. The point was that Mao left an ambiguous legacy, as he had been a contradiction himself: a strange amalgam of radical ideology and pragmatic politics. He had envisioned transformation of China into a communist society in his lifetime. But in his long march to power he had shown himself to be a consummate

practioner of political realism, making alliances or breaking
them and zigzagging his course left and right based on tactical
necessities. It was his political agility, as much as his charis-
matic appeal, that had enabled him to survive—and succeed—
in the rough-and-tumble waters of Chinese politics. Shortly
after his death, his followers would split a hair over a phraseol-
ogy attributed to him, disputing whether the chairman intended the country to be led according to "the principles laid
down," or according to "the past directives"—that is to say,
according to Mao's principles or practices.

The radicals, who formed around Mao's wife, Chiang
Ching, stressed fidelity to Mao's principles. They were the
unrepentant remnants of the Cultural Revolution Left. The
Revolution had catapulted them to prominent position at the
national level. Wang Hung-wen, a Shanghai radical, had
reached the second-ranking position in the CCP (Chinese
Communist Party) hierarchy. Chang Chun-chiao, another
Shanghai radical, had become a deputy premier. And Yao
Wen-yuan, a third prominent member of the Shanghai radical
group, controlled the state-ruled media. During the last years
of Chairman Mao's life, they had wielded powerful influence.
They had mounted the anti-Confucius campaign of 1974,
which was believed to have been directed against Premier
Chou En-lai, whose courteous manners betokened madarin
virtues, and they drove Teng Hsiao-ping out of power following Chou's death.

The Cultural Revolution, the main thrust of which was to
destroy elitism in any form, had created such confusion
throughout the country that it was followed by severe back-
lashes. Sensing the reaction, the radicals were determined to
persevere in their course. Wang Hung-wen, speaking before
the 10th Party Congress in August 1973, declared: "We must
have the revolutionary spirit of daring to go against the tide.
... When confronted with issues that concern the line and the
overall situation, a true Communist must act without any
selfish considerations and dare to go against the tide, not
fearing either removal from his post, expulsion from the party,
imprisonment, divorce nor guillotine."

In contrast to the radicals, the moderates were a diffuse
group of civil and military officials who held strategic positions

at the central and regional levels. Many of them had been subjected to personal harassment during the Cultural Revolution and restored to high positions when the furor that had been kicked up by the Revolution subsided. They were the powers in the military and in important civilian ministries. In the succession struggle their problem was essentially how to defend their positions against the ideological assaults mounted by the radicals. With Chou dead and Teng out of power, the moderates rallied behind Premier Hua Kuo-feng, who had been handpicked by Mao as a compromise candidate acceptable to both camps.

The Rise of Hua Kuo-feng   Hua Guofeng

An intimation that Hua had been chosen to lead post-Mao China came, at first, with his appointment as acting premier to succeed Chou En-lai. Knowledge of this appointment came indirectly through an official Hsinhua News Agency dispatch of Feb. 7, which said: "Hua Kuo-feng, acting premier of the State Council," the Chinese Cabinet, had met with a visiting official from Venezuela. Hua, prior to that appointment, had been a sixth-ranked deputy premier in his 60s.

The appointment was greeted with surprise by Western diplomats, scholars and, reportedly, even Chinese Communist representatives with Western contacts. In the wake of Chou's death, eulogized Jan. 15 by senior Deputy Premier Teng Hsiao-ping, it had been widely anticipated that Teng would accede to Chou's post. Following his rehabilitation in 1973, Teng had proceeded to take over the functions of the premier's office during Chou's long illness and was the chief Chinese official during U.S. President Gerald R. Ford's state visit in December 1975.

Teng's accession to power had been blocked by an intra-party split in which Mao's wife, Chiang Ching, was believed to have played a major role. Indicative of Chiang Ching's involvement in the anti-Teng drive, or "anti-rightist campaign," was an article in *Jenmin Jih Pao* (*People's Daily*), which accused "unrepentant capitalist roaders" of criticizing the operations of Hsiao Chin Chuang, a village near Tientsin in the north, with which Chiang was closely associated. The article said that this "rightist" faction had charged that Chiang's model village had received state subsidies, while it fell short of the norms set by the national model village at Tachai in Shansi Province. Additionally, Peking newspapers March 4 assailed Teng for his alleged opposition to Chiang Ching's post-Cultural Revolution cultural projects, including revolutionary operas and ballets. Teng, who was not identified in the reports, was said to have "given the green light to feudal, bourgeois and revisionist literature and art."

Among those passed over for the leadership positions were the following deputy premiers, in order of ranking: Chang Chun-chiao, a key figure in Shanghai during the Cultural Revolution; Li Hsien-nien, China's top economic specialist, regarded generally as a moderate; Chen Hsi-lien, the Peking military region commander; and Chi Teng-kuei, a party administrator.

At the time of his appointment as acting premier, Hua Kuo-feng was virtually a mystery man to most Western observers. Little was known about him outside China other than the fact that Hua spoke the Hunanese dialect and could therefore communicate with the ailing chairman better than most other people in Peking had been able to. Biographical data on him were not available. He was thought to have been born in Shansi province in northwestern China between 1915 and 1920. Chinese Nationalist sources cited by the *New York Times* Oct. 12 placed his early party career in the Liuliang Mountains of Shansi, where he served as party secretary of Kiaocheng county.

The first confirmed record of Hua's political career was in 1955, when he wrote an article for *Hsueh Hsi (Study)*, the Chinese Communist Party's theoretical journal. The article was titled "Fully Study the Dynamic Situation of Various Rural Strata." It supported Mao's campaign for agricultural collectivization. In the article, Hua claimed that his district—Siangtan in Hunan Province, of which we was party committee secretary—had collectivized 11% of its peasant families.

In 1956, Hua was elected to the party committee in Hunan, and in 1958 he was named deputy governor of the province. In that capacity, he was Hunan's ranking official, because the nominal governor was a disgraced former Kuomintang officer. During Hua's tenure as deputy governor, he became a member of a group associated with Mao's Great Leap Forward program, to modernize China's industrial production methods.

Fragmentary evidence suggested that Hua had come under some light attack by the Red Guards during the Cultural Revolution, the *New York Times* reported Oct. 13. In 1967, Hua was named deputy director of a preparatory committee that had been created to organize a revolutionary committee in Hunan. In 1969, at the ninth party congress, Hua was elected to the Central Committee. When the Hunan Province party committee was reestablished in 1970 after the Cultural Revolution, Hua was named the committee first secretary, or leader.

Hua went to Peking in 1971 to investigate a report that the late Marshal Lin Piao was plotting a coup. Hua's nomination to the investigating committee increased his prestige in party circles, and in 1973 he was elected to the 21-member Politburo, the party's main decision-making body.

In 1974, Hua presided over an agricultural delegation to Tibet, and delivered the major speech at the agricultural conference. In the speech, he warned that there were some "leading cadres on the county committees who are weak in struggle, absent-minded and lazy." As a result of his speech, wall posters appeared in Peking in June 1974 attacking Hua for repressing militant radicals in Hunan.

In January 1975, the National People's Congress, presided over by late Premier Chou En-lai, named Hua deputy premier and minister of public security. Teng's ouster in April removed the obstacle to Hua's assumption of full premiership. According to Wu Teh, the mayor of Peking, "Chairman Mao personally proposed Comrade Hua Kuo-feng for the posts of first vice chairman of the Communist Party Central Committee and prime minister of the State Council in April 1976. Then, on April 30, Chairman Mao wrote to Comrade Hua in his own handwriting, 'With you in charge, I am at ease.' "

Hua lost no time in broadcasting his international exposure. He played host to former President and Mrs. Richard M. Nixon when they visited China Feb. 21-29, 1976 at the invitation of the Chinese government to commemorate the fourth

anniversary of their historic visit to China in 1972. During his
stopover in Peking Feb 21-26, Nixon met three times with Hua.
At the banquet honoring the Nixons Feb. 22, Hua praised
Nixon's "farsightedness" in breaking the deadlock over improved ties between the two countries in 1972. He also assailed
the Soviet Union for its alleged "rabid expansionism" and
urged heightened "vigilance" on the part of the world's peoples
in order to prepare against the war threat it posed.

On the domestic campaign to criticize alleged "capitalist
roaders" in the party, Hua said that "a revolutionary mass
debate" was underway "in such circles as education, science
and technology." He characterized it as "a deepening of the
Great Proletarian Cultural Revolution" of the 1960s.

Then came Hua's formal succession to the mantle of Chairman Mao in October 1976. A spokesman of the CCP
announced Oct. 12 that Hua had succeeded Mao as chairman
of the Chinese Communist Party. The announcement followd
the appearance in Peking Oct. 9 of wall posters exhorting
citizens to "resolutely support the resolution concerning the
appointment of Comrade Hua Kuo-feng as chairman of the
party Central Committee of the People's Republic of China."

The government spokesman said Hua would also succeed
Mao as chairman of the Military Affairs Commission and
would retain—for the present—his post as premier. The
appointments thus gave Hua the three highest posts in the
government. The spokesman also said that Hua would be
general editor of Mao's collected works.

The delay in formally announcing Hua's appointment was
attributed by the party spokesman to the need to inform all
local and provincial party committees of the decision. Little
was known about how the decision was reached. The 176
members of the party Central Committee had met in Peking
for discussions after Mao's funeral, the *Washington Post*
reported Oct. 10. Many of them remained in Peking and were
still meeting to discuss the changes, the *New York Times*
reported Oct. 13.

Before the appointment was confirmed, an editorial in the
three leading Chinese newspapers had called for allegiance to

"the party Central Committee headed by Comrade Hua Kuo-feng." The editorial also enjoined citizens from promoting political feuds. "Anyone who betrays Marxism-Leninism-Mao Tse-tung and tampers with Chairman Mao's directives, and anyone who practices revisionism, divisionism and engages in conspiracy is bound to fail," the editorial said. The article also told citizens to study Mao's work.

Attack on the "Gang of Four"

The elevation of Hua to the CCP chairmanship represented a dramatic assertion of power on the part of the moderates against the radicals. On the day the official CCP spokesman announced Hua's new position, the London *Times* learned that Mao's widow, Chiang Ching, and four other members of the radical faction had been purged Oct. 7. These members were identified as Wang Hung-wen, Chang Chun-chiao, Yao Wen-yuan and Mao Yuan-hsin, Mao's nephew. Three different embassies received similar reports that day, Oct. 12, according to the *New York Times* report of Oct. 13. Later reports omitted Mao Yuan-hsin from the list of the purged radicals. The others—Chiang, Wang, Chang and Yao—ulitmately were referred to in frequent denunciatory statements as the "Gang of Four."

As many as 30 additional arrests were reported by the London *Times* Oct. 14. A number of student radicals also were arrested Oct. 13, the Oct. 14 London *Daily Telegraph* reported.

Sources said that the arrests were linked to an attempted forgery of Mao's will. It was not known whether the alleged conspirators had been accused of attempting to forge the entire will or whether they had been arrested for using a quotation, attributed to Mao but reportedly manufactured, calling for the Chinese to "act according to the principles laid down."

A report in the Oct. 14 *New York Times* cited foreign visitors as having seen wall posters around Tsinghua University and Peking University opposing Hua's nomination as chairman. The posters reportedly accused Hua of refusing to use the controversial saying in memorial services for Mao Sept. 18.

The reports did not state whether any of the purged leftists had been imprisoned or executed, nor was there any mention of violence. There were no details of the reported coup attempt.

The first official mention of the coup attempt came Oct. 19 in an editorial appearing in *Jenmin Jih Pao*, the party newspaper. The editorial attacked, but did not name, four radical leaders who had attempted to "usurp party and state power." Ostensibly a memorial article commemorating the 40th anniversary of the death of the noted writer and theorist Lu Hsun, the editorial said that Lu had been particularly critical of "enemies [and] maggots that had sneaked into the revolutionary camp." The article added that Lu had also attacked "sham Marxist swindlers [who] pursued their own selfish interests in the name of revolution..., those who speak high-sounding words in the daytime while playing tricks of creating dissension, instigating and splitting at night."

The broadcast announcement and editorial followed a nationwide poster and provincial radio campaign identifying the "Gang of Four" and denouncing them as "maggots" and "capitalist roaders." The poster campaign accused Chiang of:

■ Plotting to kill Mao Tse-tung while Mao was on his deathbed. A poster that appeared Oct. 18 on the campus of Peking University was titled "The Towering Crimes of the Gang of Four." It said, "When Chairman Mao's illness reached its crisis, Chiang Ching disregarded opposition and obstacles from the doctor and insisted on moving Chairman Mao in a vain attempt to kill him."

■ Attempting to kill Hua and to take over the government during the eight-day mourning period following Mao's death.

■ Nagging Mao "almost to death" during the final weeks of his life.

■ Attempting, with the complicity of Wang, Chang, Yao and Ma Tien-shui, a Shanghai administrator, to take over Shanghai harbor, the city radio station and other key locations in Shanghai.

■ Linking herself and her co-conspirators to the Soviet Union, which was a treasonable offense in China.

The posters led to demonstrations Oct. 15-18 by an estimated 10,000 persons in the former radical stronghold of

Shanghai. The demonstrators pasted up wall posters denouncing the four alleged conspirators and shouted such slogans as "Smash the head of the four dogs," Agence France-Presse reported.

The first official announcement of the action taken against the "Gang of Four," naming Chiang Ching and her three alleged co-conspirators, came Oct. 22 through Hsinhua, the official Chinese news agency. The announcement, made over the Peking radio, said that the Chinese Communist Party Central Committee, under Hua Kuo-feng's leadership, had crushed a coup attempt by Mao Tse-tung's widow and three other members of the party's radical faction, namely, Wang Hung-wen, Chang Chun-chiao and Yao Wen-yuan. The Central Committee, according to the announcement, had "adopted resolute and decisive measures to crush the counterrevolutionary conspiratorial clique and liquidated a bane inside the party."

The official version of the radical plot against the Hua Kuo-feng leadership was further elaborated in wall posters that appeared in Shanghai and Peking. The contents of these posters were reported in the Western press Oct. 30 and Nov. 8. According to the Oct. 30 report, the four radicals had been arrested after a gunman, acting on their behalf, had fired Oct. 6 at a convoy of cars in Peking in which Chairman Hua was riding. Four security guards were said to have been killed before the gunman and other attackers were subdued. Hua called a meeting of the Politburo later that day and ordered the arrest of the four after Chiang reportedly produced a forged document in which her late husband was purported to have designated her as his successor.

According to the Nov. 8 account, Shanghai posters reported that two days after the arrest of the four radicals, their supporters in that city mobilized and armed 30,000 militiamen in preparation for an armed uprising against the Peking regime. Plans for the insurrection were abandoned by Oct. 13 after a group of Shanghai radicals led by Ma Tien-shui, a city government official, realized that the moderates under Hua's leadership were firmly in control in Peking and that further resistance was pointless.

Jenmin Jih Pao charged Nov. 2 that Chiang and her three associates had "carried out criminal activities to energetically disrupt" the country's industrial production and to interfere in the management of its economy. The newspaper called on Chinese workers to "make up for the loss of production inflicted by the Gang of Four."

The official Chinese sources confirmed, a year later, that the arrest of the "Gang of Four" had taken place Oct. 6, 1976. In the months following the arrest, accusations against the purged radicals animated the official Chinese press. An editorial printed jointly Oct. 25 in the party paper *Jenmin Jih Pao*, the army paper *Chieh Fang Chun Pao* and the party theoretical journal *Hung Chi*, accused the four leftists of following an "ultra-right line" and of betraying national secrets. The article also said that Mao had warned in 1974 that Chiang had "wild ambitions" to succeed him. Mao had told the four purged radicals on four different occasions—July 17, 1974, Dec. 24, 1974, April 1975, and May 3, 1975—not to "form a small faction of four people," according to the article. The reference to betraying national secrets was apparently a reference to a series of interviews that Chiang Ching had given to an American scholar, Roxane Witke, in August 1972.

In another article *Jenmin Jih Pao* Dec. 18 accused the four of having reworded a critical quotation by Mao and of publishing it Sept. 16, a week after the chairman's death, to make it appear that they alone were to assume his powers. The quotation was contained in a remark Mao had made April 30 to Hua Kuo-feng, then first deputy chairman of the party. It was in response to how to conduct a campaign against Teng Hsiao-ping, ousted deputy premier. The article also accused the four of having attempted, shortly after Mao's death, to use the name of the General Office of the Central Committee to order the party committees in the provinces and cities to report directly to them. Their aim, the newspaper said, was to "sever the communications between the Central Committee headed by Hua Kuo-feng and the localities." The function of the General Office was to transmit high-level party communication. Starting Sept. 12, three days after Mao's death, Yao Wen-yuan had "time and again arranged for people to write to Chiang Ching their 'oath of fealty' " and had urged that she be named party chairman, *Jenmin Jih Pao* said.

According to another accusation leveled by the newspaper, Chang Chung-chiao had drawn up a plan soon after Mao's death on how to seize power. A *Jenmin Jih Pao* editorial Dec. 23 called the four "active counterrevolutionaries," a term implying misdeeds that deserved the death penalty. The statement said that "military and civilians of the whole country must beat the dog in the water to continue to expose and criticize the Wang-Chang-Chiang-Yao antiparty clique to the end." The term "beat the dog in the water" meant finishing off one's enemies. The editorial intimated that the "Gang of Four" faced possible execution.

Rally for Hua

In a concerted move to buttress the new chairman, the moderates began to mount pro-Hua demonstrations. *Jenmin Jih Pao* Oct. 17 reported that the Peking garrison of the People's Liberation Army had sworn to win new victories under the Central Committee headed by Chairman Hua. In Nanking and Shenyang, headquarters of two of the most important regional commands, military commanders and troops pledged Oct. 19 to support Hua and denounced those "who tamper with directives of Mao, who make revisionism, splits and plots."

An estimated one million demonstrators Oct. 23-24 celebrated the elevation of Hua as successor to Mao Tse-tung in two Peking rallies televised throughout China and around the world. The Oct. 24 rally, which followed a week of demonstrations in Peking, Shanghai and other cities, marked the first time Hua had appeared in public since he gave the eulogy at the conclusion of the mourning period for Mao. Hua did not speak at the rally. He waved from the reviewing stand at Tien An Men Square and chanted with the crowd. Standing with Hua were Yeh Chien-ying, the minister of defense, Li Hsien-nien, the first deputy premier, and Chen Hsi-lien, commander of the Peking military region. Hsinhua, the official press agency, ranked them as the three highest government officials after Hua, the *New York Times* reported Oct. 25.

Wu Teh, mayor of Peking, gave the principal address at the 80-minute Oct. 24 rally. Wu told the crowd that Hua had been "selected by our great leader Mao himself as his successor." Wu said that Mao's widow, Chiang Ching, and the three other purged members of the Politburo, Wang Hung-wen, Chang Chun-chiao and Yao Wen-yuan, had "refused to heed what Chairman Mao said" concerning his successor. The radicals "plotted and conspired tirelessly to overthrow a large number of leading comrades in the party, government and army and [to] usurp party and state leadership," Wu said. He also accused the four of "maintaining illicit foreign relations, [and] engaging in flagrant activities of capitulationism and national betrayal."

Other speakers at the Oct. 24 rally also accused the four of "attempting to attack our beloved Prime Minister Chou En-lai."

Violence Spreads

A Chinese official who spoke with visiting foreign correspondents June 5, 1977, asserted that the arrest of Chiang Ching and her co-conspirators had ended the government unrest that had begun in 1974. This official reported that the dissidents had organized militia at 10 factories in Nanchang, the capital of Kiangsi province. At one tractor station they beat up workers and halted production for 21 months. The violence did not cease with the arrest of the "Gang of Four," however. On the contrary, it sparked open rebellion in various parts of the country.

Armed clashes occurred in Fukien Oct. 27, 1976. According to reports from China Nov. 23, Chairman Hua sent troops to quell factional unrest. Broadcasts from Fukien said that People's Liberation Army units had moved into the province and had "organized large numbers of commanders and fighters into propaganda and mass work teams and dispatched them to various cities, rural villages, factories, mines, government offices and neighborhoods . . . to vigorously support local work and enthusiastically propagate the instructions of the party central committee." One broadcast said that Hua had gone to

Fukien to "investigate the work...and had made important instructions accordingly."

Chiang Ching and her three disgraced colleagues were held responsible for much of the trouble by "poking their noses into Fukien and instructing a very small number of people to practice revisionism and splittism, to engage in conspiracies and stir up bourgeoise factionalism," the broadcast said. Travelers from Fukien had reported seeing wall posters there announcing that several radicals had been arrested by Liao Chih-kao, the provincial leader. Liao had been physically attacked earlier in the year by a mob at his headquarters in Foochow, the provincial capital.

The report on the Fukien turmoil coincided with a government call Nov. 23 for obedience to central authority. The admonition, contained in a *Chieh Fang Chun Pao (Liberation Army Daily)* article, quoted a dictum of Friedrich Engels, a founder of communism. It said: "Authority is preconditioned by subordination" and "victory can be achieved only by marching in step and obeying orders. Common knowledge tells us that without authority and obedience, machines cannot be set in motion, trains cannot run and steamships cannot navigate."

In Shanghai, according to an official account made public May 17, 1977, Chang Chun-chiao, one of the four purged leaders, had mobilized militia the day after Mao's death. Six million rounds of ammunition were said to have been issued to the troops in preparation for what was intended to be a nationwide rebellion. Peking, however, moved quickly to change the Shanghai leadership. After the arrest of the "Gang of Four," Peking announced Oct. 30 the appointment of Su Chen-hua and two others as the new party leaders of Shanghai. The announcement of their designation was coupled with confirmation of the dismissal of Chiang's three associates—Chang, Yao and Wang—"from all their posts inside and outside the party in Shanghai." Su, who became mayor, held the official titles of first secretary of the Shanghai Municipal Party Committee and chairman of the Municipal Revolutionary Committee. The two other appointees were Ni Chih-fu, second secretary of the Municipal Party Committee and first vice chairman of the Revolutionary Committee, and Peng Chung, party leader of neighboring Kiangsu Province, third secretary of the Municipal Party Committee and second vice chairman of the Revolutionary Committee.

Violence was also reported in the provinces of Hupei, Honan, Shansi and Yunan in the closing months of 1976.

Broadcasts Dec. 8-9 said that Wuhan, Hupei's main industrial center, had been "thrown into chaos." The unrest prompted Hua Kuo-feng and the Communist Party's Central Committee to summon provincial officials to Peking for consultations. One radio report said the Chiang's followers in Wuhan had "organized a so-called 'second armed forces' " and had "created white terror, split the ranks of the working class, incited armed struggle [and] killed and wounded class brothers." A rally held by Hupei leaders Dec. 6 had focused on the crimes of a member of the party committee, identified in some wall posters as Chao Hsui, the provincial party secretary, according to a Wuhan broadcast.

Jenmin Jih Pao, the Communist Party newspaper, said Dec. 7 that the "Gang of Four's" operatives in Honan had "stormed the organs of the dictatorship of the proletariat and the provincial and lower-level committees." In Wuhan they had "stormed offices in charge of industry, agriculture, commerce and communications and transport," a broadcast said. Chiang's followers had carried out similar attacks in Yunan, where they "dragged out" several officials from their offices, according to a broadcast monitored Dec. 9. The broadcast said the fighting in Yunan was continuing because "the Gang of Four's influence and remnant poison in politics, ideology and organization has not yet been eliminated." Further internecine strife attributed to the radical four was reported Dec. 20 in the northern city of Paoting and Dec. 31 in Szechwan Province to the south. The reports indicated neither the specific cause of the disturbances nor the identity of those involved. Following intervention by government troops, a Chinese official said Dec. 30 that armed conflict in Paoting was lessening.

An article in the Dec. 20 issue of *Jenmin Jih Pao*, the first report of the Paoting rioting, said that radicals were causing the violent outbreaks as part of a plot by Chiang Ching and her three colleagues to sieze power. The newspaper reported "beating, smashing, looting," the destruction of military equipment and factories and the theft of state funds. Other sources Dec. 29 confirmed that military arsenals in the city had been raided, factories blown up, grain stores and shops looted and banks robbed. The violence was said to have prevented the shipment of relief material to quake-stricken Tangshan. *Jenmin Jih Pao* had reported earlier in December that the disgraced four radicals had spread discontent in Paoting and had also attempted to disrupt other parts of Hopeh Province.

A sketchy account of the fighting in Szechwan, in which lives were reported lost, was given Dec. 31 by a provincial broadcast. It accused Chiang and her three followers of inciting "civil war and factionalism" that "did not cease." It was not clear whether the fighting was continuing. The broadcast quoted speakers at a rally Dec. 24 as having said that "precious lives of many class brothers were sacrificed" in the disturbances. Another rally in the city of Ipin assailed the radicals for inciting "all-round civil war" with loss of life and property, the broadcast said. The report charged that the radicals had "squeezed out" peasant associations and seized some Communist Youth League organizations and had attempted to "deceive, seduce and poison some youths to die for them."

Moving Toward Purges

Amidst the growing political unrest, the Chinese government Dec. 2 decided to dismiss Foreign Minister Chiao Kuanhua and replace him with Huang Hua. Huang had been head of China's delegation to the United Nations since Peking was admitted to the world body in 1971. He had previously served as ambassador to Ghana, Egypt and Canada. A Hsinhua announcement Dec. 3 gave no reason for Chiao's ouster but said that Deputy Premier Li Hsien-nien had made an "explanatory statement" at the committee meeting, the first in nearly two years. Chiao reportedly had been linked to the "Gang of Four." Hsinhua said "other appointments and removals" were also decided on at the conclusion of the committee's three-day session. The only other appointment made public was that of Teng Ying-chiao, widow of Chou En-lai, who was named one of the chairmen of the Standing Committee. Teng's appointment had first been proposed by the Central Committee of the Communist Party and had been approved by Chairman Mao Tse-tung in October 1975, Hsinhua said. No reason was given for the delay in making the actual appointment.

Hsinhua said that Teng had lauded Huang's appointment as foreign minister in an address at the committee session. She said that Huang "possesses great proletarian mettle and far-sightedness." Other speakers said that Huang was "boundlessly loyal" to Mao and that he had already made "immortal contributions" to the party.

At this time, there was apparently internal debate going on at the highest echelons of the Chinese government on how to deal with the radicals who had been associated with the "Gang of Four." A *Jenmin Jih Pao* editorial Nov. 28 appealed for moderation. In dealing with the backers of the purged radicals, the editorial said, "We should allow them to correct their mistakes. We should not strike them down once and for all as the 'Gang of Four' did with the people."

"As far as comrades who have made mistakes are concerned, including those who have made serious mistakes, you should implement Chairman Mao's historical teaching, 'Cure the sickness to save the patient,' " the editorial said.

Wang had been accused by *Jenmin Jih Pao* Nov. 24 of having stirred up political strife in Hangchow, site of factional violence that had been quashed by the army in 1975.

The government's call for easing the campaign against the followers of the "Gang of Four" contrasted with an appeal the previous week by *Chieh Fang Chun Pao* (*Liberation Army Daily*) for a continuation of that drive. The army paper had demanded an "all-out people's war" to "settle accounts thoroughly" with them and their backers. "To be benevolent with them would be a crime against the people," the journal said.

Toward the end of December the Chinese government changed its tune. In an address at an agricultural conference Dec. 24, Chairman Hua Kuo-feng predicted that a nationwide purge would be carried out in 1977. "The Central Committee," he declared, "is going to launch a movement of consolidation and rectification throughout the party at an opportune time" in

1977. "The central task for 1977," he asserted, would be a continued drive against the purged four and their adherents. Hua charged that before the four were purged, they had recruited and promoted party members in violation of the Communist Party charter. "Even bad elements were drawn into the party and infiltrated into leading bodies," he said. Chiang and her associates, Hua contended, had "decked themselves out as leftists" but were actually ultra-rightists. Their downfall had forestalled a civil war and had prevented them from "capitulating to imperialism and social imperialism," Hua said, the latter two forces being a reference to the Soviet Union and the U.S.

The Return of Teng Hsiao-Ping

Call for Teng's Rehabilitation

By the beginning of 1977, it seems that disturbances in various parts of the country had, for the most part, been brought under control. An official of the Chinese government was quoted Jan. 4 as having said that "current foreign press stories about present unrest in the provinces are totally groundless." However, the Chinese official press the same day published more details of the violent incidents in Fukien Province, first reported in November 1976. The Communist Party newspaper *Jenmin Jih Pao* told of "beating, smashing and looting" in the province, where about 12,000 troops had been mobilized. The newspaper report acknowledged that the fighting had halted the operations of some factories. The newspaper blamed the turbulence on a few people who were instigated by Chiang Ching and her three colleagues to establish illegal contacts, create splits and "stir up struggles with force."

On Jan. 8, the first anniversary of Chou En-lai's death, thousands of people gathered at the Tien An Men Square in Peking to pay tribute to the late premier. There was no interference from the police as there had been in April the year before. In a wall poster that appeared in the capital that day, charges were levelled against Peking mayor Wu Teh. It attacked him for his role in the Tien An Men incident of April 5, 1976. It was Wu who had ordered the police to disperse the crowd that had come to lay wreaths in Chou's memory and blamed Teng Hsiao-ping for the disturbances that followed.

Meanwhile, a number of posters asking for Teng's rehabilitation appeared in Peking. The first such poster appeared Jan. 6. A Jan. 7 poster recalled that when Teng was in power, the "revolutionary situation was great,...everyone was in high spirits." Another placard, dated Jan. 8 and signed "Revolutionary Successor," described Teng as "a very good comrade" and asserted that he had been unfairly blamed by Chiang Ching and her colleagues for the April 5 incident. The four, it said, had used the incident to "smear the name of Comrade Teng."

45

The wall poster campaign for Teng's rehabilitation continued Jan. 9-11. Placards posted Jan. 9 assailed Wu Teh along with Chen Hsi-lien, commander of the city's military garrison, for their role in the April 1976 riots. Both men were accused of "clinging to the coattails" of Chiang Ching and her three disgraced colleagues. Wall posters Jan. 10 revealed for the first time that an undisclosed number of persons had been killed in the April disturbances. The placards appealed to Chairman Hua Kuo-feng to "reverse the verdict of the incident," otherwise "the souls of the martyrs who died on April 5 will beat drums and shed tears against false charges laid against them." Banners displayed in the city Jan. 10 accused a third Peking official, public security chief Liu Chuan-hsin, of being "responsible for the blood-shedding."

It was reported Jan. 13 that a directive issued by the Communist Party's Central Committee indicated that Teng might already be at work again in the State Council (cabinet). The Hong Kong newspaper *Ming Pao* reported that Teng had been named premier and that the appointment would be confirmed by a directive later in January. The Central News Agency of Taiwan reported Jan. 13 that Chinese Nationalist intelligence sources were in possession of a Communist directive confirming Teng's reinstatement to the State Council but making no mention of his appointment as premier.

Peking, however, kept a lid on the news about power shifts in the high echelons of the Chinese government. An official government spokesman Jan. 24 denied a report that Teng would soon be nominated first deputy chairman of the Communist Party. But unofficial Chinese sources in Peking were reported Jan. 23 to have said that Teng would soon be rehabilitated and named to the post.

Meanwhile, another step in the eventual reinstatement of Teng had been indicated when an official publication suggested Jan. 20 that the drive against him had been called off. The monthly magazine *China Reconstructs* published a new version of a speech made by Peking Mayor Wu Teh at a rally in October 1976. The new, revised version of the Wu speech omitted all criticism of Teng. Wu had said in one of the deleted passages that the people should "continue to criticize Teng

Hsiao-ping and repulse the right deviationist attempt to reverse correct verdicts."

'Deepen the Exposure of the Gang of Four'

Indicative also of Teng Hsiao-ping's growing influence in 1977 was the stepping up of the campaign against the radicals or those who had associated with them. Gone was the counsel of restraint that had been heard in the previous year. *Hung Chi* (*Red Flag*) Feb. 5, 1977 criticized the efforts of some leaders for their insufficiently harsh campaign against Chiang and her colleagues. It said: "The movement has still developed unevenly... some comrades do not fully recognize the seriousness of this struggle and hold that the 'Gang of Four' have been overthrown, have very few supporters among the people and can no longer stir up trouble."

The Chinese government Feb. 7 called for greater discipline, indicating that some areas of the nation were not following instructions of Chairman Hua Kuo-feng to "bring about great order." The statement was made in a joint editorial appearing in the Communist Party newspaper *Jenmin Jih Pao*, *Chieh Fang Chun Pao* and *Hung Chi*. The editorial reflected an apparent stepped-up campaign against Chiang Ching and her three ousted colleagues. It said, "To deepen the exposure of the 'Gang of Four' is the main theme and the key link at present." The Chinese were urged to pay heed to the principles of discipline outlined in speeches made by the late Mao Tse-tung in 1956 and by Hua Dec. 25, 1976. Hua was quoted as having stressed in his address the "strategic policy decision to grasp the key link and bring about great order in the country."

The news agency Hsinhua announced Feb. 26, 1977 that Chairman Hua had opened a new drive to improve the efficiency of the army and to end the practice of putting politics ahead of military know-how. According to an editorial appearing in *Chieh Fang Chun Pao* (*Liberation Army Daily*) and *Jenmin Jih Pao*, Hua and Defense Minister Yeh Chien-ying had "decided to launch an extensive mass movement for the army to learn" from the Sixth Company, which was described as a model army unit. The editorial lauded the company because it "adheres to rigid requirements in training and is always in combat readiness." The model unit, the statement said, avoided "the stuff peddled by the Gang of Four." The campaign represented the first changeover in the armed forces since Hua was named to head the military commission of the party's Central Committee in October 1976.

The call to "deepen the exposure of the Gang of Four" was attended by purges, at the central and local levels, that further consolidated the power of moderates throughout the country.

A broadcast from Kunming, Yunnan Feb. 12 announced a major shift in the administration of the province, including the removal of Chia Chi-yun as Communist Party chief. He was replaced by An Ping-sheng, former Communist Party head of neighboring Kwangsi Province. Yunnan had been swept by factional unrest in late 1976. In his new post, An held the titles of Yunnan Province party committee first secretary, Yunnan Revolutionary Committee chairman, first commissar of the provincial military district and first commissar of the Kunming military region, which included Yunnan and Kweichow provinces. Chia had been accused in wall posters in Yunnan in 1976 of being a follower of Teng Hsiao-ping.

In another Yunnan changeover, Chen Pi-hsien, who had been purged in the 1967 Cultural Revolution, was rehabilitated and named party secretary and deputy chairman of the Yunnan Revolutionary Committee. Prior to his ouster for "oppressing the workers' movement," Chen had served as chairman of the Shanghai Revolutionary Committee and first secretary of the city's party committee.

The decision for the Yunnan shift had been made at a top-level meeting of Communist Party Chairman Hua and Yunnan Province leaders summoned to Peking, the Kunming broadcast said. The broadcast alluded to the possible continuation of the factional strife in the province. It said that "although Yunnan now faces rather a lot of difficulties due to the interference and sabotage" by Chiang Ching and her three purged leftist colleagues, the party's Central Committee believed that with the new appointments the province "can surely overcome all problems."

Chinese authorities executed a number of persons accused of political and common crimes, it was reported March 12 and 17, 1977. Several of those put to death had been convicted of involvement in the political upheavals and widespread provincial unrest in 1976. Travelers from Hangchow March 12 quoted an official proclamation posted in the city saying that nine "class enemies" had been shot for doing "mad things." According to the placards, some of the accused had printed leaflets urging resistance to Chairman Hua and his new administration. Twenty-nine persons had been executed in Shanghai and Canton, it was reported March 17. The Shanghai Supreme Court had sentenced 26 to death as "active counter-revolutionary" criminals. Of this number, only two were found guilty of political crimes. One reportedly had impeded criticism of the "Gang of Four," and the other was said to have opposed the policy of sending educated youths to work in the countryside. The Shanghai court suspended the death sentences of 17 others and placed them on two year's probation. The three other executions, of men convicted of espionage, were carried out in Canton. Travelers returning to Peking March 2 reported seeing posters in the central industrial city of Wuhan in February stating that nine persons were sentenced to death for political and common-law crimes.

Three unidentified Chekiang officials had been put on display March 2 in the main public stadium of Hangchow, the province capital, while nearly 100,000 spectators shouted insults, according to a province broadcast. Party Chairman Hua was reported to have turned one of the three over to the people for criticism. The disgraced official was identified as the "trusted follower" of the purged "Gang of Four."

The Chinese government named new Communist Party chiefs in Heilungkiang, Chekiang and Kiangsu provinces, it was reported March 4. Promotions to other top party, military and local administrative posts also were made in the three provinces. An administrative shakeup in Kweichow Province was announced March 6 in a broadcast from Kweiyang, the provincial capital. Ma Li, a deputy Communist Party secretary in northern Hopei Province, was named party governor and head military commissar of Kweichow. The fate of the province's former party leader, Lu Jui-kin, was a mystery. He had not made a reported public appearance in Kweichow in two years, but he had been seen in neighboring Yunnan Province during that time in his capacity as deputy commander of the regional army command.

A rally of 3,000 persons was held in Kweiyang March 5 to convey "the important instruction and decision of Chairman Hua and the party Central Committee on the work of Kweichow," according to the Kweiyang broadcast. The broadcast said that since the ouster of Chiang Ching and her disgraced colleagues, "Kweichow has great prospects."

The Kwiechow shift brought to six the number of provinces affected by party shakeups in the one-month period.

Jenmin Jih Pao March 9 accused a "sworn follower" of Chiang Ching and her three deposed colleagues of having attempted to take control of the Chinese Academy of Sciences by discrediting senior academics at the institution by means of "bugging and adopting tricks of special agents." The "sworn follower" presumably was Liu Chung-yang, purged assistant secretary general of the academy. He had been accused of trying to oust his political enemies at the academy by falsely labeling them supporters of the "right deviationist line" of Teng Hsiao-ping. Chiang and her three associates also were accused of being so preoccupied with witch-hunting activities at the academy's seismological bureau that they ignored predictions of the July 1976 earthquake in Tangshan.

In a related development, a broadcast March 9, 1977 from Anhwei Province indicated the rehabilitation of two leading educators purged in 1976. The broadcast said that Chiang Nan-hsiang, former president of Peking's Tsinghua University, and Liu Ping, the school's chancellor, had been placed beside senior party leaders on the funeral list of a provincial administrator. The two men had supported Teng Hsiao-ping's educational policies, which placed more stress on hard work and less on ideology.

A crackdown against Liaoning Province officials opposed to central government policy was reported March 17. A broadcast from Liaoning said a provincial official who was a leading sympathiser of Chiang Ching and her disgraced colleagues had been arrested at a "struggle" rally March 14. Several other provincial officials, also allied with the "Gang of Four," had been "ferreted" out at another meeting held by Politburo member Li Teh-sheng, regional military commander, according to the broadcast. Indicating that the political unrest still prevailed, the broadcast said that the resolution of the "Liaoning question is not complete, we will not call off the battle until victory is won." The arrested man, identified as Chang Tieh-sheng, was said to have plotted with his associates against Peking's senior leadership in collusion with the "Gang of Four" and its supporters. The action against Chang and the others, the broadcast said, had been carried out on the specific orders of Communist Party Chairman Hua. The Communist Party newspaper *Jenmin Jih Pao* disclosed June 24 that a campaign was under way to criticize the "Gang of Four" and their "fanatic follower" in Liaoning Province, Mao Yuan-hsin, a nephew of Mao Tse-tung. The younger Mao had held important posts in the party and on Liaoning's provincial revolutionary committee and also had served as political commissar of the Shenyang military region. The newspaper article carried the headline: "Bury the Gang of Four and Bring Down the Liaoning Tyrant [Mao Yuan-hsin]."

While the radical faction was being weeded out at all levels of government and party, the restoration of the moderates was under way. An estimated 300 to 600 persons who had been arrested April 5, 1976 in connection with the Tien An Men incident were set free, according to reports from Peking March 18, 1977. Posters welcoming them appeared on the walls of Peking University, Tsinghua Technical University and on factory walls: "Warmly welcome the return of the people arrested in Tien An Men Square."

A Kansu broadcast June 22, 1977 said that province chief Hsien Heng-han had been dismissed for his alleged failure to strongly pursue the government's purge policy. He was replaced by Sung Ping as the province's new first party secretary. Sung previously had been an ordinary party secretary. Hsien's additional post as first political commissar of the Lanchow railway bureau was given to Gen. Hsiao Hua. The broadcast asserted that the influence of the "radicals" had "paralyzed" the bureau. The agency operated the railroads that connected Peking with Sinkiang Province on the Soviet frontier. The statement said that under Hsien's leadership, false information and erroneous statistics had been issued, causing "very great harm."

In an Anhwei shakeup, Sung Pei-ching was replaced by Wan Li as party chief, according to a provincial radio broadcast. A former railway minister, Wan had been elevated to the province leadership June 23. Describing conditions in Anhwei during the past eight months, the broadcast said that "the masses in the province have not been given free rein" because of "mistakes by the former principal leading person of the provincial Party Committee," an obvious reference to Sung.

The provincial purges followed a call June 6 by the commander of the Kiangsi Provincial Military District for a continuing campaign against "bad elements" in the country. Hsin Chun-chieh was quoted as having said at a rally in Nanchang, the capital: "We must certainly kill a very small number of the most vicious enemies against whom there is irrefutable evidence." The rally was held to denounce the purged "Gang of Four" and their followers in Kiangsi. Those at the gathering were informed that "four ringleaders" of the Chiang faction in the province had been arrested and "dealt with according to law." A Hupei Province broadcast June 8 told of "some leaders" there "who said or did wrong things while under the influence of the Gang of Four [and] have not even today, corrected their attitude." The statement admitted that "disunity exists in some leadership groups."

Resumption of Modernization Drive

The political unrest in the wake of Mao's death had worked to the detriment of China's economic growth. There were widespread incidents of work stoppage, sabotage and paralysis of governmental functions, especially in those provinces where factional strife raged for many months. Agricultural production in 1976-77 remained at the 1973-74 level. Industrial productivity, according to one estimate declined by 5% in 1976. China had to purchase 1.2 million tons of wheat from Australia—700,000 tons in January and 500,000 tons in November. An additional purchase of 27.9 bushels of wheat from Canada in December 1976 was also reported.

China's economic decline due to political instability was also reflected in its external trade relations with Japan. The Japan External Trade Organization reported Feb. 15 that Japan's trade with China had dropped 20% between 1975 and 1976, to $3.03 billion. According to the report, Japan's 1976 trade with China constituted 22% to 23% of Peking's entire trade with foreign nations, down from 26.7% in 1975. Japan's trade surplus with China in 1976 had totaled $291 million, a drop from the $727 million registered the previous year. Japan's exports to China in 1976 had fallen 26.4% to $1.662 billion on a customs-clearance basis, largely because of a reduction in the shipment of chemical fertilizers and machinery, the trade group said.

Reports from China portrayed a troubled economy. A wall poster appearing in Canton pointed out major shortcomings in China's economy and noted that it had been far surpassed by Japan's in the past 10 years, it was reported Feb. 1, 1977 by foreign travelers arriving from the city. The 20-page document complained of China's low standard of living, the breakdown of social order and an increase in crime. It cited the slowdown of economic development in the past decade, "especially the production of consumer goods." The placard boasted of the inherent superiority of the socialist system, while blaming China's economic problems on Chiang Ching and her purged radical colleagues. Because of their influence when they held power, "mass enthusiasm was lost and production was damaged." While noting that Japan produced more steel, automobiles and rice than China, the poster rejected the idea that the Chinese were "inferior to the Japanese people in intelligence." The poster called for reforms to restore economic health. The reforms sought included "measures so the workers can organize production and participate in controlling socialist property" and an increase in the standard of living and establishment of "a rational system of wages and incentives." The poster, whose authorship was not known, was signed "worker."

Later in the month, *Hung Chi* (*Red Flag*), the CCP's doctrinal journal, came out in favor of selective private production, largely in the fields of agriculture and handicrafts. It said that these "legal family occupations carried out on the side" would help diversify products, which would then be sold to the state for market distribution. The proceeds would then be used to develop light industries. *Hung Chi's* appeal reversed a previous official press policy of discouraging all types of "private" activities. The article, headed "It is well to take care of the well-being of the masses," said that the policy of accelerating economic growth since the downfall of Chiang Ching must also be applied to the manufacturer of consumer goods. It called for a greater output of such products as cotton, sugar, salt and bicycles.

The Communist Party newspaper *Jenmin Jih Pao* March 11, 1977 called for a major effort to bolster China's ailing economy, which it said was plagued by serious energy, food and industrial shortages. Asserting that "problems should not be hidden from the masses," the newspaper spoke of "temporary difficulties in industrial production" and coal supplies. Ten million persons had been mobilized to cope with a serious drought in Shantung Province, where "the situation continues to worsen, seriously affecting the normal growth of wheat," *Jenmin Jih Pao* reported. According to a Radio Peking broadcast, the Communist Party Committee in the province had convened emergency meetings to map plans to save the winter wheat crop; 31,000 new irrigation wells had been sunk in the previous few months.

A campaign of "rigid economy" in the consumption of coal, oil and electricity had been urged. "We must send every ounce of coal, every watt of electricity and every drop of oil we have to places it is most needed in revolution and production," *Jenmin Jih Pao* said.

Scattered reports told of persistent disaffection among the people. Travelers from Shanghai said March 11 that they had seen posters on the walls of the Municipal Revolutionary

Committee building demanding higher wages. A Fukien Province broadcast quoted delegates at a local conference as saying that individual farming, speculation and profiteering in the province had not yet been eliminated.

At this time, many sections of southern and northeastern China were in the grip of the country's worst drought since 1949, according to official reports March 18-21. The drought posed a threat to the growth of summer-harvest crops and to the spring sowing. Grain rations were reported being cut in some of the hard-hit areas. A broadcast from southern Kwangtung March 21 said the prolonged dry period in the province was "developing daily, seriously threatening the smooth progress of spring farming." With no heavy rain since November 1976, water levels in some areas were close to the lowest ever recorded, the broadcast said. Reporting on a meeting of provincial leaders March 18, the broadcast reported that a call had been issued to "mobilize the masses to carry, store, and transport water, resist drought, crash-plant and protect the rice seedlings." Similar conditions were reported in Shansi, Shensi, Honan, Hupei and Shantung provinces. A circular issued March 20 by the central government's State Council (cabinet) said the drought was "extremely severe in areas along the Yellow and Huai rivers and a number of plains in northern China." It said that there had been no snow or rain in many of these places for half a year. Honan Province had mobilized 14 million persons and Shantung 17.5 million to haul water from rivers and reservoirs to wheat fields, according to the reports. The most seriously affected crops in the north were wheat and barley sown during the winter and scheduled to be harvested in June and July. A government statement carried in *Jenmin Jih Pao* March 24 advised factories, schools, offices and army units to release their personnel immediately so that they could join bucket brigades.

A dispatch from Hong Kong March 25 said that the *New Evening Post*, a Communist-supported newspaper there, had reported a "tense situation" with regard to the food supply in Chekiang, Kiangsi, Fukien, Szechwan, Yunnan and Kweichow provinces. Factional strife had been reported in many of those areas in 1976. The newspaper speculated that official exaggeration of "the actual statistics" might have been one factor leading to the food shortages. It said: "Production was not all that abundant, yet they increased their figures.... Thus the state took its share of the grain according to the exaggerated figure. It looked like there was enough left for the people to eat, but in reality there was not."

Against this background the Chinese government resumed the drive for the modernization of agriculture, industry, national defense and science and technology—a program referred to as the four modernizations. The plan for China's modernization in the above four areas had been outlined by the late Premier Chou En-lai in his keynote address to the Fourth National People's Congress, which had met Jan. 13-18, 1975. According to the plan, China was to build a "relatively comprehensive industrial and economic system" in the decade of 1976-85 and join the rank of advanced industrial nations by the year 2000. The progress toward Chou's ambitious goals had been handicapped by the factional strife between the radicals and moderates. The defeat of the radicals, however, presumably eliminated the main political obstacle to the modernization drive.

Hsinhua, the Chinese official news agency, reported Feb. 6, 1977 that four separate but related conferences were being held in Peking. Communist Party Chairman Hua Kuo-feng and other high-ranking officials had received 800 conference delegates in Peking, the report said. The four conferences dealt with air defense, the work of defense plants under the Third Ministry of Machine Building, defense planning and military research and production. The delegates to the sessions had pledged to "push forward the defense industry and research work and strive for modernization of national defense and science and technology," according to Hsinhua.

Western experts who had visited China had reported that its armed forces were equipped with outdated weapons from the 1950s. The experts, confirming Western intelligence reports, had said that the Chinese were especially short of advanced anti-tank and anti-aircraft missiles and related electronic equipment.

An expanded conference designed to mobilize the masses for accelerated industrial production was convened April 20 at Taching, located in Heilungkiang province. Called "the National Industrial Conference," it was opened by CCP Chairman Hua Kuo-feng. The conference moved to Peking April 27. The gathering of 7,000 to 10,000 delegates represented all sectors of industry, commerce and communications throughout the country.

Speaking at the opening ceremony, Deputy Premier Li Hsien-nien urged "a race against time to build China into a powerful, modern socialist country." He stressed the need to "greatly speed up China's industrial growth and economic strength and national defense capacity" in preparation for what he said was "a world war" that was "bound to break out some day." Defense Minister Yeh Chien-ying told the conference session in Peking May 9 of the importance of building up China's defense forces, with emphasis on the manufacture of steel. Without steel, he said, "we will not have enough modern arms and equipment" and other necessities of war. In excerpts of his address published May 13, Yeh also said that the U.S.-Soviet rivalry could lead to "a big war at an early date." He reiterated that China's defense industry was engaged in "a race against time."

Hsinhua, the official Chinese news agency, said that China was about to launch a "new leap forward" to develop a modern economy, according to the *Asian Wall Street Journal* May 4. "The scale and impact of the new leap forward is expected to top that of the 1958 leap," Hsinhua said.

Along the same line, the Chinese government had announced April 11, 1977 that China was gradually recovering from the economic difficulties resulting from the 1976 factional strife. The statement, appearing in *Jenmin Jih Pao*, cited an eight-point plan of Chairman Hua for bolstering the government leadership, the economy and the army. Hua had "given us a magnificent blueprint for grasping the key link in running the country well ... by giving us these eight points." a *Jenmin Jih Pao* editorial said. "By following this strategic policy decision and grand plan mapped out by Chairman Hua, we can certainly administer China's affairs well and build China . . . into a more powerful country." Among the eight points listed were a call to continue the anti-leftist drive, a demand for reorganization of the Communist Party and a call to bolster the army. The army guidelines re-emphasized the recent plan for modernization. It said: "We must effectively strengthen preparedness against war and military training, learn military skills, [and] raise combat strength. . . . " The editorial said that if China worked hard, it might attain "initial success within this year and great success in three years' time."

The *New York Times* June 9 reported the establishment of the second major oil export terminal in little more than a year in Liaoning Province in the area formerly known as Manchuria. The new port was located at Dairen (Talien). It was reported that it would be capable of servicing oil tankers of up to 100,000 tons. Its completion was announced in May in a Chinese broadcast picked up by a U.S. government monitoring service.

The *Financial Times* (London) said July 13, 1977 that according to official Chinese figures, the growth rate in the oil industry as a whole had fallen to 12.7% in the first three months of 1976, compared to 25% in the first half of 1975, and an average of 20% annually in previous years. The Taching field, known to be the richest in the country, was increasing production at an 11.3% rate instead of the 18.7% annual average it had maintained since 1966.

The new drive was hailed as a success by the official Chinese sources. The press agency Hsinhua claimed that "the fast rate of recovery of China's economy since the overthrow of the Gang of Four has exceeded all estimates," it was reported July 15. Hsinhua said that despite political upheavals in 1976, industrial production in January-June 1977 showed an increase over the same period of the previous year. Hsinhua indicated that the pickup had occurred in the previous two or three months when output of most of the major manufacturing industries "met or topped monthly targets and many of them hit all-time highs." As in previous Chinese economic reports, few specific figures were given. Petroleum showed the largest gain, with production going up 10.6% over the first half of

1976. Coal, iron and steel, electric power and the railroads, the industries hardest hit by the 1976 upheavals, also showed improvement, Hsinhua said. According to the press agency, the coal industry had "fulfilled its half-yearly targets 21 days ahead of schedule," and the "record for average daily output of electric power was time and again improved in the second quarter."

Reinstallation of Teng

Culminating the process that established the moderate control of the Chinese government was the official announcement of Teng Hsiao-ping's reinstallation as deputy premier. The announcement, made in the name of the Chinese Communist Party Central Committee, first appeared in Peking wall posters July 19, 1977 and was confirmed in the official communique of the Chinese government July 22. The announcement also contained the news that the "Gang of Four"—Chiang Ching, Wang Hung-wen, Chang Chun-chiao and Yao Wen-yuan—had been expelled from the party.

The news of Teng's reinstallation did not come as a surprise, as Hua Kuo-feng had suggested in March that the CCP Central Committee come to an official decision to permit Teng to "resume work." The Central Committee's official action restored to Teng all the official positions he had held at the time of his removal in April 1976; he was reinstalled as deputy premier, chief of staff of the General Staff of the army, a member of the Central Committee of the committee's Politburo and of its Standing Committee and deputy chairman of the Military Commission of the Central Committee. In reassuming his role in government, Teng was ranked behind Chairman Hua and Yeh Chien-ying, a deputy chairman and defense minister. The communique reaffirmed Hua as successor to Mao Tse-tung.

With regard to the four ousted members, the communique reiterated charges of conspiratorial activities that previously had been leveled at them, including an attempt to overthrow Premier Chou En-lai in 1973. The four disgraced officials, the statement said, were "a counterrevolutionary conspiratorial clique. They completely opposed the basic principles ('practice Marxism and not revisionism; unite and don't split; be open and aboveboard, and don't intrigue and conspire'), engaged in conspiratorial activities aimed at splitting the party and usurping party and state power."

The resolution adopted by the plenary session said that the party, people and the army were "more united, the dictatorship of the proletariat is more consolidated,...and a new leap forward is taking shape in the national economy."

Chinese Thermidore

The 11th Party Congress

Teng's ascendancy reflected a gravitation of power toward the old guard. Within less than a year after Mao's death, the radicals followed the "Gang of Four" into political oblivion. It appeared that the new regime was led by a triumvirate made up of party Chairman Hua Kuo-feng and two deputy chairmen, Defense Minister Yeh Chien-ying and Deputy Premier Teng Hsiao-ping. Yeh was 79 years of age and Teng in his eighties. Another strong man of the new regime was Wang Tung-hsing, who had been the head of Mao's elite bodyguards and had played an important role in the downfall of the "Gang of Four."

By the summer of 1977 the moderates, now back in power, had completed preparations to hold another party congress to ratify the changes made since the arrest of the "Gang of Four." The 11th Congress of the Chinese Communist Party met in Peking Aug. 12-18. The 1,510 delegates, representing 35 million members of the party, assembled in Peking's Great Hall of the People. They heard reports by Chairman Hua, Defense Minister Yeh and Deputy Premier Teng. The official communique said: "The reports... were conscienciously and warmly discussed by the Congress. The minds of the delagates were at ease and they spoke freely." The Hong Kong-based *China News Analysis* reported: "In the intervals they had probably been well entertained; the province cadres and workers had a grand time in Peking."

In an address to the delegates Aug. 12, Chairman Hua said the purge in 1976 of the party's radicals "marks the triumphant conclusion of our first Great Proletariat Cultural Revolution, which lasted 11 years." In summarizing the chairman's address, Hsinhua quoted him as saying, "Now... we are able to achieve stability and unity and attain great order across the land in compliance with Chairman Mao's instructions."

The Party Congress adopted a new Party Constitution, the text of which was published by Hsinhua Aug. 23. The docu-

ment had been introduced Aug. 13 by Defense Minister Yeh
Chien-ying, who said it was vital to "let the masses say what is
on their minds." One article specifically provided members
with the right to criticize party organizations and officials and
to take their appeals as high as Chairman Hua. The new
constitution stressed discipline but also encouraged more open
discussion within the party. It emphasized eonomic development as a major goal and contained provisions aimed at preventing further eruptions of political factionalism. The charter
required all new party members to serve on probation for a
year, a move interpreted as an attempt to prevent the infiltration of radicals. The party should foster conditions "in which
there are both centralism and democracy, both discipline and
freedom, both unity of will and personal ease of mind and
liveliness," the document declared.

In addition, the Party Congress elected a new Central Committee of 201 regular members and 132 alternates. Some of
them were veteran officials who had not been included in the
last Central Committee, chosen in 1969 and 1973. One committee member was Lo Jui-ching, a former chief of staff of the
armed forces who had been purged during the Cultural Revolution in the 1960s.

The new Politburo had 26 members—23 regulars and three
alternates. The regular members were Hua Kuo-feng, Teng
Hsiao-ping, Yeh Chien-ying, Li Hsien-nien, Wang Tung-
hsing, Wei Kuo-ching, Unlanfu, Fang Yi, Liu Po-cheng, Hsu
Shih-yu, Chi Teng-kuei, Su Chen-hua, Li Teh-sheng, Wu Teh,
Yu Chiu-li, Chang Ting-fa, Chen Yung-kuei, Chen Hsi-lien,
Keng Piao, Neih Jung-chen, Ni Chih-fu, Hsu Hsiang-chien
and Peng Chung. Eleven of the 26 had military backgrounds
and seven were military commanders or political commissars.

At the head of the Politburo was a five-man standing committee, which consisted of the triumvirate plus two other men:
Li Hsien-nien and Wang Tung-hsing. Li was a veteran financial expert who had served as a deputy premier under Premier
Chou En-lai. He was in his eighties. The five men constituted
the Presidium of the 11th Party Congress.

Modification of Mao's Credo

In 1966, ten years before Mao's death, Chairman Mao had written in a letter to his wife, Chiang Ching: "After me the right wing will take power, for the time being... They will use my words to confirm their evil power... But they will not rule long...." Post-Mao developments were said to confirm Mao's prediction. His erstwhile colleagues, who had been overshadowed by him during his life, refused to remain servile to his memory after his death. To be sure, they continued to pay lip service to his thought, but they began making changes that constituted departures from Mao's policies, especially those established during the Cultural Revolution.

On the first anniversary of his death, Sept. 9, 1977, a huge mausoleum containing the body of Mao Tse-tung was opened in Peking. Among the officials attending a brief ceremony marking the occasion was Lo Jui-ching, former chief of staff of the People's Liberation Army, who had been purged during the Cultural Revolution. (Lo had been rehabilitated in 1975 and was a member of the CCP military commission.) Chairman Hua Kuo-feng, who delivered the principal address, called on the Chinese people to "hold high the great banner of Chairman Mao and carry out his behest."

The anniversary of Mao's death, however, was marked, more significantly, by a call for modification of his credo. A turning away from the late chairman's dogma was urged by Politburo member Nieh Jung-chen in an article appearing in the theoretical journal *Hung Chi* (*Red Flag*). Nieh's remarks, broadcast earlier in the week, suggested that the new leadership should be guided by its own pragmatism in developing China's industry and that it should not feel bound by Mao's policy of placing greater emphasis on social concerns rather than on economic problems. "To correctly apply Mao thought, we must master its spiritual essence, study its stand, views and methods, regard its basic theories as our guide to action, and firmly combat the tendencies to make use of a number of phrases... as dogma in order to disregard time, location and

conditions," Nieh said. In urging a more practical approach to
China's problems, Nieh noted that "the objective world is full
of contradictions and changes." As a result, he said, "our
thinking must realistically reflect such contradictions and
changes." Nieh warned that "if the leading cadres satisfy themselves with general calls and with a few quotations as the basis
for such calls, they will not be able to solve problems."

Nieh's article was followed by the publication Sept. 10 of a
joint editorial in China's three leading newspapers: *Jenmin Jih
Pao* (*People's Daily*), *Chiehfang Chun Pao* (*Liberation Army
Daily*) and the party's theoretical journal, *Hung Chi* (*Red
Flag*). The editorial accused the "Gang of Four" of having
quoted Chairman Mao's works out of context, distorting their
meanings. "We must not," said the editorial, "mechanically
apply stray quotations from Chairman Mao's works in disregard of the correct time, place and circumstances. Statements
made on a particular question at different times and in different circumstances may sometimes differ." Mao himself, the
article continued, had "criticized certain people who 'regard
odd quotations from Marxist-Leninist works as a ready-made
panacea which, once acquired, can easily cure all maladies.' "

The return to normality brought a sense of relief to Chinese
intelligentsia. The books that had been banned during the
Cultural Revolution were back in circulation. Bans was lifted
from Western music; one could play Beethoven. (*Jenmin Jih
Pao* pointed out that Lenin had liked Beethoven.) Teachers
and writers were accorded traditional respect, no longer subjected to the kind of personal humiliation and harrassment
they had been put through in the days of the Cultural Revolution. One western analyst characterized China's intellectual
scene as "cultural liberation."

In this relaxed intellectual-political climate, the CCP leadership placed great emphasis on science. The Party Central
Committee Sept. 18 issued a circular, made public by the
Hsinhua news agency Sept. 22, saying that it planned to con-
vene a national science congress in Peking in the spring of 1978.
The purpose of the parley would be to promote the modernization of science and technology as a means of achieving the
modernization goals set by the late Premier Chou En-lai for the

year 2000. The circular accused the "Gang of Four" of having interfered with the progress of science and technology. The disgraced radicals "were opposed to study of Western advanced technology and at the same time killed off initiative in our country," the circular charged. Moreover, it continued, the "Gang of Four" engaged in "willful persecution of intellectuals and the suppression of views expressed on academic matters." During their period in office, some research laboratories had been closed and laboratory equipment destroyed.

In an effort to reverse the trend, the CCP Central Committee proposed a thorough discussion of what had been done under the aegis of the "Gang of Four." In addition, it decided to take concrete steps to upgrade the country's scientific research. There steps were to include the establishment of a State Science & Technology Committee; the establishment of research organization, and the convening of scientific conferences at the regional and national levels. Lest this new push for science become an elitist enterprise, the circular referred to Chairman Mao's triple revolution: class struggle, production struggle and scientific experiment. Scientists would not work alone in their laboratories but in unison with the masses, the Central Committe decreed. Scientific work would spread through "the four-grade agricultural science network" in rural communes and "the organization of technical innovation in factories and mines."

According to foreign specialists in Hong Kong, the Central Committee's statement appeared to reflect a reversal of the policies of Mao or those carried out in his name, which, in the opinion of some foreign observers, had set back Chinese science by a decade. During the Cultural Revolution, Mao had required that scientists spend much of their time in farms or factories, and he had insisted that their work be practical, rather than theoretical.

A further indication of a departure from Maoism was evident in a major educational reform that the Chinese government announced Oct. 21; it required colleges to give entrance examinations and permitted some high school students to go directly to college without having to work several years in the countryside. The new program reversed some of the key

changes Mao had made during the Cultural Revolution. Mao
had sought to make the educational system more egalitarian
and to eliminate what he regarded as useless academic practices. The late chairman believed that a student's political
attitude was a more important prerequisite for college admission than his grades. Critics had charged that Mao's policies
lowered educational standards, depriving China of well-
trained graduates to meet its needs.

The new educational program was announced by the Hsinhua news agency, which said it had been adopted at a national
conference held by the Education Ministry. Hsinhua conceded
that educational deficiencies of the past few years had caused a
sharp downturn in the output of scientists and technicians.
According to Hsinhua, universities and colleges were being
told that they should start postgraduate courses before the end
of the year to train specialized, highly skilled research workers.
Hsinhua Oct. 24 disclosed the concern expressed by Chinese
officials over a drop in the educational level of their schools. In
Shanghai, for example, a test had recently been given at a
university to graduates working in scientific and technical jobs.
Some 68% failed in mathematics, 70% in physics and 76% in
chemistry. The test, the agency said, was based on high-school
level course requirements.

Return to Discipline

The prolonged political instability worked to the detriment
of the country's economic development plans. Nevertheless,
according to the Paris-based Organization for Economic
Cooperation & Development (OECD), China had expanded
its economy in the past 25 years at "an impressive rate." In a
report released Aug. 16, 1977, the OECD stated that China's
annual increase in gross national product in the past 20 years
ranged between 4% and 6%. Considering China's "size and
complexity of problems," the country's economic expansion
was described in the report as "impressive." The most impressive feature in China's economic performance" was its industrial growth. The OECD report attributed this to "fairly
large-scale periodic infusions of foreign technology and capital

goods." The report predicted that China's growth rate would expand 3% to 5% annually in the near future, "assuming no political or economic disasters" occurred.

The OECD's estimates appeared to be contradicted by a report, released Aug. 15, of the U.S. Central Intelligence Agency. Forecasting a mixed economic outlook for the immediate future, the CIA study noted that economic development was particularly linked to agriculture and modernization of industrial technology. This kind of program, the report noted, called for heavy investments, increased imports, management reforms and incentives to improve worker efficiency. According to CIA Deputy Director Sayre Stevens, China's "new leaders are aware that this means modifying some of the Cultural Revolution's reforms, which were hostile to rapid economic progress, and they will give greater stress to higher academic standards and scientific and technological competence."

In another account of China's economy, a publication of the Bank of America had reported Aug. 11 that Peking had registered a $762-million trade surplus in 1976 with non-Communist countries. The report, contained in the journal *China Spotlight*, quoted Western sources as saying that imports in 1976 had fallen nearly 25% from a year earlier to $4.91 billion while exports had risen 2% to $5.67 billion. This compared with trade deficits of $455 million in 1975 and $810 million in 1974, the report said. Japan's total trade with China in 1976 had dropped 20% to $3.04 billion, but Tokyo remained Peking's principal trading partner. Hong Kong was second, and the U.S. fell to sixth from fifth with a trade total of $336 million.

In an effort to increase industrial productivity, China's State Planning Commission called for tighter economic controls. The commission Sept. 12 published a major review of its economic policy. In this paper it urged increased centralization, greater industrial profits and production and more imports of Western technology. The statement said that the government was re-establishing six major regional economic zones with responsibility for coordinating development in the provinces. This system had been used in the late 1950s but was later dropped by Mao Tse-tung.

The commission apparently had decided not to increase wages. This was indicated in passages that said factory officials should "restrict bourgeois rights," and "the masses should be encouraged to take a Communist approach toward work." The term "bourgeois rights" as used in Peking included material incentives. "The socialist principle of 'from each according to his ability and to each according to his work' should be consistently applied," the commission declared. This meant factory wage differentials would be continued.

In stressing the need for centralization as opposed to decentralization, the commission reaffirmed the government's authority over a wide scope of industrial activities. These included distributing raw materials to industry, setting wages and regulating the number of workers.

Paralleling the move toward the restoration of centralized control in China's economy, the government strengthened its control over the armed forces. The Hsinhua news agency Sept. 25 reported the appointment of Wei Kuo-ching as the director of the armed forces' political department. Wei was a member of the CCP Politburo and a close associate of Teng Hsiao-ping's. Wei's appointment to the position formerly held by Chang Chun-chiao, a member of the discredited "Gang of Four," was viewed as an attempt to deal firmly with the residual influence of the radicals in the armed forces.

The announcement of Wei's appointment came closely on the heels of the publication by Hsinhua Sept. 19 of an article by Politburo member Hsu Hsiang-chien. In his article, the author charged that factional strife in China in recent years had led to a breakdown of discipline in the armed forces. Hsu disclosed that some army officers and men had disobeyed orders for supposed political reasons. Calling on the armed forces to return to the Communist principles of discipline and honesty, Hsu asked, "How can the army fight a battle if everyone acts according to his own will and wishes?" The army was "investigating every person and every matter in the army connected" with the purge of radicals after Mao Tse-tung's death, Hsu said. Referring to the abandonment of self-control in view of the factional strife, Hsu complained: "Some people interpreted their superiors' orders and directives out of context and used them for their own purposes." He criticized those who "think they can drive a bargain over a superior's orders and do not have to resolutely execute them."

Hsu's article was another in a series of recent Chinese statements calling for the restoration of discipline. In his article earlier in September, Politburo member Nieh Jung-chen had urged the Chinese to "revive and carry forward our party's fine tradition of seeking truth from facts, of being honest, talking honestly and working honestly."

Meanwhile, there were reports of continued political unrest in various regions of China and of harsh crackdowns. An official broadcast from Kwangsi Chuan Autonomous Region Sept. 22, 1977 indicated political dissent in the region. A Sept. 26 report from Hong Kong, where the broadcast was monitored, said the official statement had called for the defense of Chairman Hua Kuo-feng's "leadership position" against "reactionary speeches" criticizing the Communist Party Central Committee. It was not clear who was opposing Hua's leadership in the region, how serious that resistance was or when it had emerged. The broadcast said: "We must spontaneously uphold, ardently propagate and resolutely defend Chairman Hua's leadership. We must deal effective blows at the kind of reactionary speeches which harm and discredit Chairman Mao's great banner and attack and split the party Central Committee headed by Chairman Hua."

Similar political unrest had been alluded to in a broadcast from Hupei Province the previous week. The broadcast complained of "ineffective leadership in some places and units. ... The masses are very dissatisfied over this."

In late October, an upsurge in political executions was reported. The *Times* of London reported Nov. 1 a steady increase in the number of persons put to death for political as well as for common-law crimes since the ouster of the "Gang of Four." This was the government's way of ridding the country of extremist influence, the *Times* held. In a late political case, 23 persons had been executed in the southwestern city of Kunming in September for subversive activites, according to the city's court proclamation seen there by travelers, it was reported Nov. 1. The defendants had been convicted of such offenses as forming counter-revolutionary groups and distributing leaflets. Twenty-four others accused of similar crimes were said to have received jail sentences. Ten persons had been executed in Peking for common crimes, according to an official poster signed by the city's Municipal Court and reported in an Agence France-Presse dispatch Oct. 29. The notice, dated Oct. 11, listed 10 others convicted of criminal offenses. In addition to those in Peking and Kunming, executions had been reported in a number of other cities, including Wuhan, Hangchow, Shanghai, Canton and Shenyang.

These accounts of executions were followed by the publication in *Jenmin Jih Pao* (*People's Daily*) Nov. 28 of an article in which China's Public Security Ministry accused the national police of employing spying and torture methods and warned against overuse of the death penalty. This ministry, which was in charge of the national police, gave an account of cases of the past 10 years in which it said disgraced members of the Communist Party and others were subjected to forced confessions and torture. "Discretion should be exercised in arresting people, and especially in executing people," the report said. The ministry quoted the late Mao Tse-tung as having said, "In cases where it is marginal to execute, under no circumstances should there be an execution and to act otherwise could be a mistake." The ministry suggested that in capital crimes that do not arouse public outcry, convicts should be granted a two-year reprieve.

A *Jenmin Jih Pao* article appearing Dec. 4 defended sentences handed down by people's courts, including the death penalty. The article was written by the "study group of the highest court of justice in Peking." It took issue with Lin Piao, the late defense minister, and the "Gang of Four" radicals purged in 1976, who had charged that the people's courts or judges were "fascists and hangmen." The article asserted that since 1949, when the Communists came to power, the people's courts had obeyed "the party line" and respected "the national laws" by applying "the sentences laid down for national traitors and counter-revolutionary elements...."

The Fifth National People's Congress

With the restoration of discipline, China's economy apparently showed an upturn. In its year-end report, released by

Hsinhua Dec. 26, 1977, the Chinese government declared that China's industrial production had increased at least 14% in 1977 and that farms had "a fairly good harvest" despite "serious natural disasters earlier in the year." Production quotas for 32 of 80 major industries were fulfilled by the end of November, and most other goals would be met by the end of the year, according to the report. It said that total industrial output in the first 11 months was 13.7% higher than in the same period of the previous year and was expected to "be over 14% by the year's end." Reporting on the country's oil production, Hsinhua said there had been an 8% increase. (Foreign analysts estimated 1976 production at about 84 million metric tons, which would mean that output in 1977 had reached almost 91 million tons if the percentage given by Hsinhua was accurate. China did not publish figures, only percentages.)

The improved economic situation provided a favorable backdrop to the convening of another National People's Congress, which would be the final step to be taken to legitimize the new regime. The Congress had been scheduled to meet in the latter part of 1977, but it had been postponed until early 1978. The Congress finally met in its fifth session in Peking Feb. 26-March 5, 1978.

Prior to the opening of the Congress, the CCP Central Committee held its preparatory meeting Feb. 18-23. A communique issued at the conclusion of the session announced the approval of the 10-year economic development plan, the revised Constitution and the new lyrics to the national anthem that were later to be adopted by the Congress meeting. The communique also said that China had returned to normal after years of factional strife. Chairman Hua Kuo-feng said, "Things are going much better than expected."

The lyrics to the new national anthem that the CCP Central Committee approved for adoption by the National People's Congress ran as follows:

> "March on, brave people of our nation,
> Our Communist Party leads us on a new Long March.
> Millions as one, march on, toward the Communist goal.
> Build our country, guard our country.
> We will work and fight.

March on, march on, march on!
Forever and ever, raising Mao Tse-tung's banner.
March on.
Raising Mao Tse-tung's banner, march on, march on,
    march on and on!"

This new anthem would replace the old one, *March of the Volunteers*, adopted in 1954, which had fallen into disfavor during the Cultural Revolution.

Following the conclusion of the CCP Central Committee's preparatory session, the preparatory session of the National People's Congress itself met Feb. 25. Soong Ching-ling, the widow of Dr. Sun Yat-sen, addressed the meeting as the senior member of the outgoing standing committee. The NPC Preparatory Session elected a 254-member presidium for the Congress and adopted the agenda for the Congress session that had been drawn up by the CCP Central Committee.

The formal opening of the National People's Congress took place Feb. 26. The 3,497 delegates, representing workers (26.7%), peasants (20.6%), soldiers (14.4%), intellectuals (15.0%), patriotic personages (8.5%), overseas Chinese (1%) and national minorities (10.9%), gathered in a large theater in the Hall of the People.

The first to address the Congress was Chairman Hua Kuo-feng, whose report lasted for three and a half hours. In his report, Hua asserted that "sabotage and interference in 1974-76" by the now-purged radical elements had resulted in a loss to China of "about 100 billion yuan in total value of industrial output, 28 million tons of steel and 40 billion yuan in state revenue, and the whole economy was on the brink of collapse." (A yuan was equal to about 61 U.S. cents.) The suppression of the radicals had brought "order" to the country and the economy "is on the path of steady growth and healthy development," Hua said.

Hua also disclosed that the government had decided to abolish the provincial revolutionary management committees formed during the Cultural Revolution to run schools, factories, and farm brigades. However, the committees would be retained at the local government level in cities, counties and other minor civil divisions. The provincial bodies would presumably be replaced by other governing bodies in China's 29 provinces.

Hua also presented China's 10-year economic development plan (1976-85), the main features of which were incorporated into the new Chinese constitution. The new economic plan envisaged that:

■ Farm output would be raised by an average 4% to 5% and industrial production at a rate of 10%. Annual steel production would be nearly tripled to 60 million tons and grain output would increase to 440 million tons a year. (The 1977 harvest was estimated at 272 million tons, and steel output for the year was estimated at 22 million tons.)

■ A total of 120 industrial complexes would be constructed. These would include 10 iron and steel plants, nine nonferrous metals centers, eight coal mines, 10 oil and gas fields, 30 power stations, six mainline railroads and five ports.

■ Eighty-five percent of major farmwork would be mechanized by 1985. Cultivated land would be expanded to an average of one mou (one-sixth of an acre) per rural resident. The current cultivated area was estimated at 500 million mou for the country's 700 million peasants.

■ Six major economic regions would be developed by 1985 to improve management. A similar system had been abolished in 1950 because the regions turned out to be too independent.

■ Factory workers and managers would receive gradual wage increases, provided the production plan was fulfilled.

Yeh Chien-ying, the outgoing defense minister and one of the triumvirates, presented the new Chinese Constitution March 1. In his speech submitting the draft, Yeh stated that it would "enshrine the great banner" of the late Mao Tse-tung. This was considered a subtle downgrading of the old charter, which, when adopted in 1975, made "Mao Tse-tung Thought" the doctrine of the state. Replacing the charter of 1975, the new Constitution was based largely on the one adopted in 1954,

China's first as a Communist state. Several articles of the 1954 document were revived, and a number of provisions of the 1975 Constitution were dropped. The right to defense in a trial was restored, and any person could file complaints against government officials. Ethnic minorities were given back their rights to "preserve or reform their own customs and ways." Among other features of the Constitution:

■ The National Congress was affirmed as the highest organ of state power, but the 1975 phrase "under the leadership of the Communist Party" was deleted. The Congress was given the power to declare war. This authority had been embodied in the 1954 Constitution and was dropped in 1975.

■ The people were granted the right to "speak out freely, air their views fully, hold great debates and write big character posters." These new rights were in addition to the ones granted in 1975, such as freedom of speech, press, and assembly, and the right to strike.

■ The rights and interests of overseas Chinese were retained, with the protection extended to relatives inside China.

■ There was to be rapid economic growth, development of education, science and technology and material incentives for workers.

■ The prosecutor offices were to be restored. Yeh Chien-ying said these agencies were being reinstated "in view of extreme importance in fighting against violations of law and discipline." (The offices had been abolished after the prosecutors attempted to punish persons for factional fighting during the Cultural Revolution.)

■ The "revolutionization and modernization" of the army would be strengthened according to Yeh. (Chinese generals had complained that the army had been weakened by neglect of training and the lack of modern weapons during the years of political turmoil.)

In its closing session March 5, the National People's Congress unanimously voted to adopt both Chairman Hua's and Marshal Yeh's reports.

The most significant outcome of the People's Congress was the reappointment of Hua Kuo-feng as premier. Hua's retention of his post, announced at the final session, came as a surprise, since it had been widely believed that he would be replaced by First Deputy Premier Teng Hsiao-ping. In recent months Hua's duties appeared to have been restricted.

Teng, who was then believed to wield the real power, thus remained the third-ranking member of the Communist Party hierarchy, behind Hua and Marshal Yeh Chien-ying, who was named by the Congress as chairman of its Standing Committee. This largely ceremonial post, vacant since the death in 1976 of Marshal Chu Te, was equivalent to head of state. Yeh's position as defense minister was taken over by Hsu Hsiang-chien, a marshal of the army.

The Congress took no action to revive the position of president, which had been abolished after its last incumbent, Liu Shao-chi, had been disgraced during the Cultural Revolution of the 1960s.

Teng's apparent predominance in government was manifested in the selection by the Congress of 13 deputy premiers and a new State Council (cabinet) that was weighted toward his political allies and programs. Five of the deputy premiers were new appointees. In addition to Defense Minister Hsu, they were: Fang Yi, a Politburo member, who headed the Chinese Academy of Sciences and the newly created State Scientific & Technological Commission; Kang Shih-en, a Central Committee member, who headed the new State Economic Commission; Chen Mu-hua, an alternate Politburo member, minister for economic relations with foreign countries, and Keng Piao, a Politburo member in charge of relations with other Communist parties.

The only incumbent deputy premier removed by the Congress was Wu Kuei-hsien, a woman textile worker who had been linked to the disgraced radicals. She had little power.

Two of Teng's closest associates were given important jobs. Hu Chiao-mu was appointed president of the newly formed Chinese Academy of Social Sciences. Sung Jen-chiung was named minister of the Seventh Ministry of Machine Building, which produced planes and missiles for the air force. Hu was a

party historian who had assisted Teng in drawing up controversial plans for economic reform in 1975. Sung had served
under Teng since the Civil War against the Nationalists in the
1940s. He had been purged during the Cultural Revolution.

The State Council was expanded to 37 ministries from 29.
The new agencies were: the State Economic Commission; the
State Scientific & Technological Commission; the Nationali-
ties Affairs Commission (which had been disbanded since the
Cultural Revolution); the Ministry of Civil Affairs (an appar-
ent replacement for the Ministry of Internal Affairs, also abol-
ished in the Cultural Revolution); the Ministry of Textile
Industry (also a former agency); the People's Bank of China,
the state central bank, which was being raised in status; the
Ministry of Chemical Industry (formed out of the Ministry of
Petroleum and Chemical Industry), and the All-China Federation of Supply & Marketing Cooperatives.

In remarks closing the Congress session, Deputy Premier
Teng said, "We have held a meeting of unity, a meeting of
victory."

Tilt to the West

Soviet Overtures Fail

Whether rightly or wrongly, Mao Tse-tung had been regarded as the main impediment to ending the Sino-Soviet dispute. His death, therefore, raised the speculation that the two largest Communist nations would be able to move closer toward each other. Moves toward rapprochement actually got under way during the last months of Mao's life.

The Soviet Union April 28, 1976, urged China to agree to the resumption of talks on the two nations' disputed frontier areas. The talks had collapsed in 1975. The Soviet request, printed in the Soviet Communist Party newspaper *Pravda*, asserted that "a package of constructive proposals from the Soviet delegation lies on the table of the Soviet-Chinese negotiations on a fronter settlement. The discussion and realization of these proposals ... could quickly take the negotiations out of their present impasse." The article conceded that the Chinese territorial claim in dispute involved only about 13,000 square miles of Soviety territory. (Moscow had asserted in the past that China claimed a total area of 600,000 square miles.) The Soviet Union, however, continued to refer to the Chinese claim as "groundless." The *Pravda* article, which was signed by I. Alexandrov—a reputed pseudonym for a high-ranking Kremlin official—blamed the Sino-Soviet conflicts on Mao Tse-tung.

One day after this proposal had been made, there was an explosion of a bomb outside the gates of the Soviet embassy in Peking before dawn April 29. The explosion killed two Chinese guards, the Soviet news agency Tass reported. There were no Soviet casualties among the embassy staff, but damage was extensive. A protest had been lodged with Chinese authorities "in connection with the incident," Tass said. The Chinese government April 30 confirmed the report of the blast, but not of the casualties. Peking blamed a "counter-revolutionary" saboteur for the incident. In Chinese political rhetoric the term "counter-revolutionary" generally was applied to pro-Soviet elements in China. This usage, press reports said, made it difficult to probe the implications of the bombing.

77

A Chinese Foreign Ministry spokesman in Peking said the matter was being investigated further. The Chinese increased security around the Soviet embassy by adding extra troops and plainclothesmen. Soviet envoys told two Western diplomats that the incident had occurred after a group of Chinese had sought admission to the embassy grounds, the *New York Times* reported May 1. At an April 30 reception, Vasily S. Tolstikov, Soviet ambassador to China, said that he had seen two persons killed and one wounded in the explosion.

Following the death of Chairman Mao, the Soviet Union stepped up its overtures to China. In an article Oct. 1 marking the 27th anniversary of the Communists' takeover of China, *Pravda* indicated the Soviets' willingness to improve relations with Peking.

Commenting on an official congratulatory note sent to Peking by the Soviet government, *Pravda* said that Sino-Soviet problems could be resolved "in the spirit of good-neighborly relations, mutual benefit and respect for each other's interests.... The fundamental interests of the Soviet and Chinese people do not clash but coincide." The article was the first lengthy Soviet press commentary on Sino-Soviet relations since the death of Mao and the first Soviet article in recent years that avoided attacking Mao's ideology.

China's responses to these Soviet overtures were not at all consistent; they showed a measure of ambivalence. In October 1976, the Soviet and Eastern European Communist parties sent congratulatory messages to Hua Kuo-feng on the occasion of his election to the chairmanship of the Chinese Communist Party. The Chinese government Oct. 28 rejected these messages. Commenting on the decision, a Chinese Foreign Ministry spokesman said, "We have no party to party relations with them." That the Chinese government had no intention of improving its relations with the Soviet Union was underscored by Deputy Premier Li Hsien-nien's speech Nov. 15 at a banquet honoring visiting President Jean-Bedel Bokassa of the Central African Republic. The Russians, said Li, "kept creating the false impression of relaxation" in Sino-Soviet relations. Earlier, Soviet Ambassador Vasily D. Tolstikov and diplomats from seven Soviet-bloc nations had walked out of the banquet in protest against other remarks by Li.

Previously, Li had told a group of visiting French journalists Nov. 2 that the Soviet Union's internal policies were marked by "fascism" and that its theory of "limited sovereignty" amounted to telling other nations "to give in and come under the Soviet big stick." He said Sino-Soviet relations would change for the better only when "the Soviets thoroughly acknowledge their faults and all the misdeeds they have committed" since Khrushchev's rise to power.

Li's sharp attack on Moscow, however, contrasted with a friendly congratulatory cable sent by Peking to the Russian leaders Nov. 7 to commemorate the 59th anniversary of the Bolshevik revolution. The statement said, "The Chinese people have always cherished their revolutionary friendship with the Soviet people."

Another conciliatory Chinese move took place at about the same time: Peking acceded to the Soviet proposal to resume border talks. Leonid Ilyichev, the chief Soviet negotiator at the Sino-Soviet negotiations on border disputes, returned to Peking Nov. 27 for the resumption of the talks. Ilyichev had declared, when he left Peking 18 months previously, that he would not return unless there was a good prospect of substantive progress. He was greeted warmly at the airport by Yu Chan, Chinese deputy foreign minister. They resumed their interrupted negotiations Nov. 30 in what was interpreted as a sign of a Sino-Soviet rapprochement under the new Chinese leadership. However, it was not long before the negotiations reached an impasse. China demanded that the Soviets remove troops stationed in the disputed areas as a condition for further negotiations and that they recognize that land occupied by Russia during Tsarist times had been seized illegally. The Soviet Union refused to concede unfair acquisition of the areas in question.

Ilyichev left Peking Feb. 28, 1977. Afterwards, the Soviet Union publicly blamed China for the impasse. A long commentary May 14 in *Pravda* attacked China for "advocat[ing] publicly and without any camouflage a new world slaughter."

It accused Peking of preparing for war against the West as well as the Soviet Union and warned the West against establishing close relations with China. The article, according to analysts, was "very tough" in comparison with a conciliatory commentary that had appeared just after Mao's death.

The U.S.S.R. announced May 26 that it had delivered a formal protest note to the Chinese embassy in Moscow, criticizing Peking for sabotaging efforts to improve Sino-Soviet relations. It was the first formal Soviet protest to China since the death of Mao, and it dispelled expectations of a consequent improvement in Sino-Soviet relations.

Impasse in Sino-American Relations

China regarded defense against the Soviet Union as taking precedence over the question of Peking's relations with the United States and the issue of China's claim to Taiwan, according to a speech attributed to Keng Piao, head of the Central Committee's International Liaison Department, it was reported Jan. 26, 1977. Keng was said to have delivered the address Aug. 24, 1976; its text was reportedly obtained and made public by Chinese Nationalist intelligence sources in Taiwan.

Although China held the U.S. and the Soviet Union to be China's enemies, the threat of Soviet aggression was so great that for the sake of survival, China must "give up one and win over the other," Keng was quoted as saying. Keng was further quoted as saying: "From the strategic point of view, if we shelve the China-United States controversy, we will be able to cope with one side with all-out effort and even gain time to solve our domestic problems first." As for China's claim to Taiwan, the text said Keng acknowledged that "even if Chinese-United States relations were normalized, it would still be impossible to liberate Taiwan immediately." Keng held that for the moment the U.S. served to moderate the Soviet threat against China. He said: "Just let the United States defend us against the influence of Soviet revisionism and guard the coast of the East China Sea so that we can have more strength to deal with the power in the north [the Soviet Union] and engage in state construction. When we regard the time as right, we will be candid and say: Please, Uncle Sam, pack up your things and go."

Taiwan remained a major stumbling block in China's rapprochement with the United States. U.S. Secretary of State Cyrus R. Vance made a trip to Peking in August 1977 to negotiate on normalization of U.S.-Chinese relations.

Prior to Vance's departure, the Carter Administration took pains to underscore its support for the Taiwan regime as well as its desire to establish diplomatic relations with Peking. A State Department official Aug. 19 said public-opinion polls and conversations with key members of Congress had convinced the Administration of strong American concern "about doing anything to appear to be abandoning Taiwan. We have no intention of doing anythng that would appear to abandon Taiwan. We want to look for ways that move forward and take account of Taiwan." According to an Administration official, President Jimmy Carter had instructed Vance before his departure to inform the Chinese that while the U.S. recognized Peking's special concern with Taiwan, the Chinese should also take into consideration Washington's historic and domestic problem that prevented the U.S. from cutting itself off from Taiwan in order to establish ties with Peking. The U.S. also was worried about the effect its repudiation of Taiwan would have on Japan and other Asian nations, the official added.

On its part, the Chinese government took a similarly unyielding public stance. Shortly before Vance's arrival in Peking, Hsinhua, the official news agency, carried Chairman Hua Kuo-feng's remarks, which read: "If the relations between the two countries are to be normalized, the U.S. must sever its so-called diplomatic relations with the Chiang (Nationalist President Chiang Ching-kuo) clique, withdraw all its armed forces and military installations from Taiwan and the Taiwan Straits area and abrogate its so-called 'mutual defense treaty' with the Chiang clique. Taiwan Province is China's sacred territory. We are determined to liberate Taiwan. When and how is entirely China's internal affair, which brooks no foreign interference whatsoever."

Vance arrived in Peking Aug. 22. Soon after his arrival, he entered into discussions with a delegation headed by Foreign Minister Huang Hua. At a dinner given later that evening in Vance's honor, Huang said, "There are still problems in the relations between our two countries," an allusion to Taiwan. Noting that China's conditions for resuming normal ties with the U.S. had not changed, Huang called attention to Chairman Hua's speech on this subject at the recently concluded 11th Congress of the Chinese Communist Party.

The American Secretary of State conferred again with Foreign Minister Huang Aug. 23, and then met with Deputy Premier Teng Hsiao-ping Aug. 24. His final meeting Aug. 25 was with Chairman Hua. Hua concurred with Vance's view, expressed throughout his visit, that the talks between the secretary and the Chinese leadership were exploratory. The chairman said his government appreciated the fact that President Carter and Secretary of State Vance had stated that Washington regarded the 1972 Shanghai communique as the basis for U.S.-Chinese relations. That communique foresaw the eventual American withdrawal from Taiwan.

At a press conference April 25, Vance said his discussions with Hua had been "candid and serious" and had "enhanced our mutual understanding." He also said that in addition to the Taiwan controversy, his meetings with the Peking leaders dealt with trade, cultural contacts, the Carter Administration's concern with human rights and U.S. military policy. A White House statement issued Aug. 25, after the conclusion of the talks, said that President Carter was "impressed with the reports he has received on the depth of the discussions between Secretary Vance and the highest officials in the Chinese government, and with the constructive attitude displayed by those officials. It is indicative of their interest in maintaining and broadening relations between the two countries."

The Chinese, however, were not pleased with the results of their talks with Secretary of State Vance. Deputy Premier Teng Hsiao-ping, in an interview with visiting Associated Press officials Sept. 6, asserted that Vance's visit had dealt a setback to the normalization of U.S.-Chinese relations. According to Teng, Vance had suggested establishing full ties with China along with an embassy but at the same time setting up a liaison office in Taipei. Teng said that this was a reversal of the current situation and was rejected by his government because it would mean continued U.S.-Taiwan diplomatic relations. This, according to Teng, represented a U.S. retreat from the position that former President Gerald R. Ford and former Secretary of State Henry A. Kissinger had taken during their visits to Peking in October and December 1975. Teng said that Ford had promised in his December meetings with Chinese officials that if he were reelected the following year, he would sever diplomatic relations with Nationalist China and establish ties with Peking. Ford, according to the deputy premier, had pledged that he would resolve the Taiwan problem as Japan had done in 1972: cutting ties with the Chinese nationalists, but maintaining nongovernmental contacts with Taiwan, including trade.

Former President Ford did not contradict Teng, but offered a slightly modified version of his conversation with Teng. In a statement issued Sept. 7, Ford said he had told the Chinese in 1975 that any American break with Taiwan in exchange for normal ties with Peking was only a "possibility." Avoiding any direct response to Teng's remarks, Ford said "any change toward normalization [of ties with Peking] must be predicated on the peaceful solution" of the Taiwan problem. Ford said he had suggested "that the Japanese solution is a possibility. I think we must continue forward movement in the normalization process" with Peking.

China Moves Closer toward Western Europe

While the normalization of Sino-American relations was being blocked by the Taiwan problem, the Chinese government scored a greater success in drawing closer toward Western Europe. China had been the first Communist country to accept the European Common Market's November 1974 offer of non-preferential commercial arrangements. This was followed by the establishment in September 1976 of formal relations with the Common Market. Shortly thereafter, the Chinese government sent a delegation to Brussels to begin negotiations for a commercial trade pact. By the spring of 1978, the negotiations had been successfully completed, and a five-year trade accord, which gave each other most-favored-nation status, was initialled in Brussels Feb. 3. This was the first trade pact between the European Community and China, although Chinese goods already had enjoyed most-favored-nation trading status in the Common Market countries.

The joint statement, released in Brussels by negotiators for both sides, said the agreement had "deep political meaning because it constitutes one of the most evident demonstrations of the excellent relations between the People's Republic of China and the community."

Acceptance of the pact had been delayed several hours because of difficulties over wording. The Chinese had resisted at first a standard Common Market trade clause that allowed either side to impose import controls on products that threatened to disrupt domestic markets. The EC had insisted on the clause to prevent the possibility of being swamped by certain Chinese exports. The Chinese also agreed to an EC demand that prices for goods traded between the EC and China would be at world market prices.

The Soviet Union sharply criticized the EC-China trade pact through press comments in Tass and *Pravda*. According to press reports Feb. 6, Tass said the talks leading to the accord had been conducted "in an anti-Soviet spirit with the aim of increasing Chinese access to European technology." Tass also charged that the agreement was "designed to achieve strategic goals." *Pravda* said Feb. 9 that China's ambitions threatened not only the Soviet Union and its allies but Western nations as well. *Pravda* added that the EC would supply China with weapons as a result of the pact.

The formal signing of the trade agreement took place April 3. Both the EC and China hailed the pact as an important step in their bilateral relations. From China's point of view, the pact definitely was aimed against the power of the Soviet Union. Chinese Foreign Trade Minister Li Chiang said, "We support Western Europe in its union for strength and in its struggle against hegemony." China's use of the word hegemony usually referred to the extension of the Soviet Union's political power.

The EC's external affairs commissioner, Wilhelm Haferkamp, welcomed Chinese support for European unity but asserted that the nonpreferential trade agreement negotiated between the EC and China was "directed against no one." The Soviet news agency Tass denounced the EC-China pact, it was reported April 4. Tass said the agreement was "opening the way for China to NATO arsenals, with the Common Market as a go-between."

Sino-Soviet Tension Increases

Later that month, the on-again-off-again border talks between China and the Soviet Union were resumed, with the arrival in Peking April 26, 1978 of the chief Soviet negotiator, Deputy Foreign Minister Leonid Ilyichev.

Hardly had the negotiations been resumed when another border incident erupted. Peking May 11 accused Soviet border troops of striking across the Ussuri River and attacking Chinese citizens. China's Hsinhua news agency said the incident had taken place May 9 at Hulin, 200 miles (320 kilometers) south of the Soviet city of Khabarovsk. According to Hsinhua, a Soviet helicopter, 18 military boats and 30 Soviet troops penetrated 2½ miles (four kilometers) into Chinese territory. "They chased and tried to round up Chinese inhabitants, shooting continually and wounding a number of them," Hsinhua reported. The Soviets were said to have "seized 14 Chinese and dragged them all the way to the [Ussuri] riverside, giving them kicks and blows." Hsinhua said the Chinese were released after "repeated protests by the Chinese inhabitants" of the area. It called the incident a "military provocation" and asserted that only Chinese restraint had prevented a renewed outbreak of hostilities such as had occurred in 1969.

Chinese Deputy Foreign Minister Yu Chan delivered a protest note May 11 to Soviet Ambassador Vasily Tolstikov in Peking. The Soviet Union May 12 apologized for the incident but claimed that the guards had crossed the border by mistake. Tass, the Soviet news agency, said that a group of border guards had been pursuing "a dangerous armed criminal" during the night and had landed on the Chinese bank of the Ussuri in the belief that they were on one of the islands in the middle of the river. Tass denied "any actions involving Chinese citizens." It asserted that when the troops discovered they were in Chinese territory, "they immediately left." It said Moscow had expressed "regrets" over the incident. Peking May 13 expressed dissatisfaction with the Soviet explanation, saying it did not "conform to reality."

At about this time another incident occurred, this time in Africa, and aggravated Sino-Soviet tension. Soviet-backed secessionist guerrillas invaded Zaire's southern Shaba Province May 11 and quickly occupied Kolwezi and Mutshatsha, two of the principal towns in the province. The guerillas were members of the National Front for the Liberation of the Congo (FNLC), a group that had invaded Shaba in March 1977. Zaire radio reported the invasion May 14, charging that the rebels, who numbered 4,000, were receiving support from Angolan and Cuban forces. In addition, Zairian President Mobutu Sese Seko accused the U.S.S.R., Algeria and Libya of backing the invasion. He requested aid from the United States and several other countries that had helped Zaire during the 1977 invasion.

Reports on the fighting were inconclusive. The FNLC May 15 said its forces had captured Kolwezi and Mutshatsha, but the Zairian government contradicted the guerrillas' claim. The U.S. State Department said May 14 that most of Kolwezi, the principal mining town in the copper-rich province, was in rebel hands. The U.S. May 16 placed airborne troops on alert for possible use in evacuating the U.S. nationals in Shaba. Fighting continued. By June 3, casualty figures for the fighting included more than 200 Zairian troops killed. In Kolwezi alone, Red Cross officials said, more than 600 bodies had been buried by May 27, including 96 Europeans and 200 Africans. (Most of the bodies were too badly decomposed to be identified.) Five members of the French Foreign Legion had been killed in the fighting.

Representatives of Belgium, France, Great Britain, West Germany and the U.S. met in Paris June 5 to discuss France's plan of creating a pan-African military force to protect pro-Western African nations from threats to their security. The participants agreed to give Zaire short-term aid but refused to adopt any long-term plans for maintaining African stability. The U.S. and Great Britain opposed the French plan. They preferred to meet individual threats to African security as they occurred and to act with the cooperation of the Organization of African Unity, in an effort to avoid East-West conflict on the continent. A communique issued at the end of the one-day meeting said the delegates had approved unspecified "recommendations to their governments." According to press reports, the recommendations included logistical support to the African troops that were patrolling Zaire and emergency financial aid to the Zairian government.

Although not included in the consultation among the Western powers that met in Paris, China came out strongly in support of Zaire. Foreign Minister Huang Hua flew to Zaire. At the end of a five-day visit, Huang promised President Mobutu June 7 that China would give Zaire full support in its "just struggle to safeguard national independence against a new aggression... by Soviet socialist imperialism." The invasion of Shaba, Huang asserted, "was an important part of Soviet policy in seeking world domination."

At this time China was also embroiled in a dispute with the Soviet-backed government in Vietnam. Against this background, another U.S. attempt was made to patch up the differences between Washington and Peking. U.S. National Security Adviser Zbigniew Brzezinski made a special visit to Peking May 20-22. Brzezinski said in a toast at a banquet given in his honor May 20 by Chinese Foreign Minister Huang that "the President of the United States desires friendly relations with a strong China. He is determined to join you in overcoming the remaining obstacles in the way of normalization of our relations." The U.S. national security adviser also said that the U.S. recognized and shared China's determination to "resist the efforts of any nation which seeks to establish global and regional hegemony." (The term hegemony was Peking's code word for Moscow's reputed attempt to dominate China.) Huang, who had conferred with Brzezinski on his arrival earlier in the day, said in his address that U.S.-Chinese ties would improve if Washington implemented the 1972 Shanghai communique.

Brzezinski May 21 held another round of talks with Huang and later met separately with Deputy Premier Teng Hsiaoping. U.S.-Chinese differences were cited by the Hsinhua news agency following talks May 22 between Brzezinski and Premier Hua Kuo-feng. It quoted Brzezinski as having said in the discussions that "even where we disagree, I believe there is an

underlying mutual respect for our separate positions." At a
banquet following his meeting with Hua, Hsinhua said, Brzezinski noted the mutual interest of the U.S. and China in
countering Soviet influence in Africa. Neither the U.S. nor
China "dispatches international marauders . . . to advance big-
power ambitions in Africa," the U.S. national security adviser
was quoted as saying. "Neither of us seeks to enforce the
political obedience of our neighbors through military force."

On completing his China visit, Brzezinski flew to Tokyo,
where he briefed Japanese officials May 23-24 on his talks in
Peking. He met with Premier Takeo Fukuda May 23 and
informed him that China was interested in resuming negotiations on a peace treaty with Japan, which had been suspended
since 1975.

The stepped-up effort toward Sino-American rapprochement brought a sharp rebuke from the Soviets. Soviet President Leonid Brezhnev denounced the U.S. June 25 for
"attempts . . . to play the 'China card' against the Soviet
Union." In a speech in Minsk, the capital of the Soviet republic
of Byelorussia, Brezhnev said the U.S. policy of improving
relations with China was "shortsighted and dangerous," and its
proponents "may live to regret it." The speech was Brezhnev's
first public reaction to a recent deterioration in U.S.-Soviet
relations. He was apparently reflecting Soviet concern over the
shift in U.S. policy toward China. As a result of Brzezinski's
visit to Peking, it was believed that the U.S. had decided to
emphasize the common concerns of China and the U.S. in
halting alleged Soviet expansionism.

Sino-Japanese Peace Treaty

The Soviet attempt to thwart China's anti-Soviet drive was
dealt yet another setback in 1978 with the conclusion of a
Sino-Japanese Treaty of Peace & Understanding. The treaty
negotiations, which had started in 1972, had been suspended in
1975 as a result of China's insistence that it contain an "anti-
hegemony" clause, opposition to a third nation's aspirations
for "hegemonism." Moscow had made it clear to the Japanese
government that the inclusion of such a clause in the Sino-
Japanese Peace Treaty would be construed as directed against
the Soviet Union.

While not accepting this Soviet interpretation, the Japanese government had tried its hand at "playing the China card" in order to secure the return of four Kurile islands that had been under Soviet occupation since the end of World War II. Japanese Foreign Minister Sunao Sonoda went to Moscow in January 1978. A round of negotiations he held with Soviet Foreign Minister Andrei Gromyko and Prime Minister Alexei Kosygin Jan. 9-10 proved to be completely unproductive. Gromyko and Kosygin expressed concern that Japan would sign the Chinese peace treaty with its "anti-hegemony" clause directed against the U.S.S.R.'s "sphere of influence in Asia." In his talks with Gromyko Jan. 9, Sonoda assured the Soviet foreign minister that the anti-hegemony clause in the proposed treaty was not directed against any third country and did not signify hostility toward Moscow. The talks failed to produce a joint communique. The Soviet Union rejected a Japanese request that a combined statement include reference to a 1973 bilateral understanding that the issue of the Kuriles was one of the problems outstanding between the two countries.

The Japanese then decided to move ahead with the conclusion of a peace treaty with China. Following Brzezinski's visit to Peking, it was announced in Tokyo June 14 that China and Japan would resume their talks on the peace treaty. This announcement brought a formal protest from the Soviet Union. In a note handed to the Japanese government June 19 by Soviet Ambassador Dmitri Polyanski, Moscow accused China of "hostility" toward the Soviet Union, "of undermining progress in detente, [and] fanning the menace of war." "Under these circumstances," the note continued, "Japan...will be linked with the diplomatic line of Peking. This would run counter to the cause of maintaining peace and security in the Far East." Japanese Premier Takeo Fukuda later June 19 rejected the Soviet warning and said that his government would continue its negotiations with Peking. "Japan's relations with China are one thing, and Japan's relations with Moscow are another thing," Fukuda said.

The Sino-Japanese negotiations resumed July 21 between delegations headed by Japan's ambassador to China, Shoji Sato, and Chinese Deputy Foreign Minister Han Nien-luang. Again, an impasse developed over the anti-hegemony clause. China insisted that any anti-hegemony clause deal specifically

with the Soviet Union. Japan, concerned about its already
strained relations with the Soviet Union, suggested a more
general reference to hegemony. To help break the impasse,
Japanese Foreign Minister Sonoda flew to Peking Aug. 8.
Under the compromise subsequently worked out, the anti-
hegemony clause stated that Japan and China "declare that
neither of them should seek hegemony in the Asia-Pacific
region or in any other region and that each is opposed to efforts
by any other country or group of countries to establish such
hegemony."

China further cleared the way for an agreement by dropping
its claim to the Senkaku Islands in the East China Sea, Sonoda
said. The island chain, also claimed by Japan and Nationalist
China, had been the scene of a near-clash in April between
armed Chinese fishing vessels and Japanese patrol boats. Sonoda said the Chinese had pledged that there would be "no
recurrence" of the incident. Sonoda also disclosed that the
Chinese had indicated to him that they would abrogate the
30-year Sino-Soviet treaty when it expired in 1980. The accord
named Japan as a threat to both nations.

A 10-year pact pledging peace and friendship was finally
signed in Peking Aug. 12, 1978 by Foreign Ministers Sonoda of
Japan and Huang Hua of China. The signing ceremonies were
attended by Chinese Communist Party Chairman Hua Kuo-
feng and Deputy Premier Teng Hsiao-ping.

Moscow responded to the signing of the treaty by charging
that its hegemony clause "is directed against the Soviet Union,
which was repeatedly noted in speeches by Peking leaders
themselves." The statement, cited by the Soviet news agency
Tass, quoted Chinese Foreign Minister Huang as saying that
common opposition to "hegemonism" was the "basis of the
Sino-Japanese treaty." Tass also criticized Japan, saying that it
had "capitulated to Peking" although Tokyo was "aware of
including into the treaty an article which is of an openly
anti-Soviet character and serves the selfish interests" of Peking's leaders.

The U.S. State Department Aug. 12 welcomed the treaty,
saying it promoted Asian peace and stability.

The Sino-Japanese Treaty of Peace & Understanding was
formally implemented as representatives of both countries

exchanged documents of ratification in Tokyo Oct. 23. The documents were exchanged by Foreign Ministers Sonoda and Huang. The ceremonies were attended by Japanese Premier Fukuda and Chinese Deputy Premier Teng, who had arrived Oct. 22. Teng said that the accord would not only enhance Chinese-Japanese political, economic and scientific relations but would also contribute to peace and stability in Asia and the rest of the world.

Teng was guest of honor at a luncheon given by Emperor Hirohito, and he conferred later in the day with Fukuda. Referring to past bitter relations between their two countries, including Japan's occupation of large regions of China before and during World War II, Hirohito said, "There have been some unfortunate incidents in the past, but I expect peace will now continue for a long period."

Text of the Treaty of Peace & Understanding

Following is the text of the Treaty of Peace & Understanding between Japan and the People's Republic of China, signed in Peking Aug. 12, 1978 and formally implemented in Tokyo Oct. 23:

Japan and the People's Republic of China, recalling with satisfaction that since the government of Japan and the government of the People's Republic of China issued a joint communique in Peking on September 29, 1972, the friendly relations between the two governments and the peoples of the two countries have developed greatly on a new basis,

Confirming that the above mentioned joint communique constitutes the basis of the relations of peace and friendship between the two countries and that the principles enunciated in the joint communique should be strictly observed,

Confirming that the principles of the charter of the United Nations should be fully respected,

Hoping to contribute to peace and stability in Asia and in the world,

For the purpose of solidifying and developing the relations of peace and friendship between the two countries,

Have resolved to conclude a Treaty of Peace and Friendship and for that purpose have appointed as their plenipotentiaries:

Japan: Minister for Foreign Affairs Sunao Sonoda
People's Republic of China: Minister of Foreign Affairs
Huang Hua
Who, having communicated to each other their full powers,
found to be in good and due form, have agreed as follows:

Article I

1. The contracting parties shall develop relations of perpetual peace and friendship between the two countries on the basis of the principles of mutual respect for sovereignty and territorial integrity, mutual nonaggression, noninterference in each other's internal affairs, equality and mutual benefit and peaceful coexistence.

2. The contracting parties confirm that, in conformity with the foregoing principles and the principles of the charter of the United Nations, they shall in their mutual relations settle all disputes by peaceful means and shall refrain from the use or threat of force.

Article II

The contracting parties declare that neither of them should seek hegemony in the Asia-Pacific region or in any other region and that each is opposed to efforts by any other country or group of countries to establish such hegemony.

Article III

The contracting parties shall, in the good neighborly and friendly spirit and in conformity with the principles of equality and mutual benefit and noninterference in each other's internal affairs, endeavor to further develop economic and cultural relations between the two countries and to promote exchanges between the peoples of the two countries.

Article IV

The present treaty shall not affect the position of either contracting party regarding its relations with third countries.

Article V

1. The present treaty shall be ratified and shall enter into force on the date of the exchange of instruments of ratification which shall take place at Tokyo. The present treaty shall remain in force for ten years and thereafter shall continue to be in force until terminated in accordance with the provisions of paragraph 2.

2. Either contracting party may, by giving one year's written notice to the other contracting party, terminate the present treaty at the end of the initial ten-year period or at any time thereafter.

In witness whereof the respective plenipotentiaries have signed the present treaty and have affixed thereto their seals.

Done in duplicate, in the Japanese and Chinese languages, both texts being equally authentic, at Peking, this twelfth day of August, 1978.

For Japan: (signed) Sunao Sonoda

For The People's Republic of China: (signed) Huang Hua

Indochinese Imbroglio

Cambodia Clashes with Vietnam

The defeat of the U.S.-backed Saigon regime in 1975 did not bring peace to Indochina; it set, instead, the stage for a new war—this time, among Communist countries.

Vietnam is situated in the geographical zone in which China, for centuries past, had held cultural and political sway. In an effort to stave off Chinese influence the newly unified Vietnam moved closer to the Soviet orbit. This caused Peking great annoyance. At the same time, the growing power of Vietnam cast a long shadow over Southeast Asia, especially over its immediate neighbors, Cambodia and Laos. Suspecting that Vietnam harbored an ambition to create, under its aegis, a federation of the three Indochinese republics, Cambodia turned to China for protection. The result was that China and the Soviet Union found themselves being drawn into a volatile situation in Indochina, where they threw their weight behind their respective protégés.

Toward the end of 1977, frequent armed clashes were reported along the Cambodian-Vietnamese borders. Hanoi radio accused Cambodia of having initiated the fighting and said that Cambodian troops had occupied large parts of Vietnam's Gialaicong Province. This was corroborated by Western intelligence sources, according to which the Cambodians had conducted a major attack in November into Vietnam's Tay Ninh Province. The Vietnamese struck early in December around Neak Luong, in Cambodia's Svay Rieng Province. The area, also known as the Parrot's Beak, was fully occupied by Hanoi's troops to a point just south of the town of Svay Rieng, the provincial capital. A report from Bangkok Dec. 24 said that fighting around Neak Luong had intensified, with the Vietnamese using warplanes and artillery. The source said that Cambodian and Vietnamese losses "appear to have been substantial" and that the combat had been waged on both sides of the frontier. Sources in Washington and Bangkok said that the scale of fighting could be on the regimental level or higher. Cambodian authorities Dec. 27 confirmed the fighting around Neak Luong but did not mention the Vietnamese by name. A Pnompenh broadcast said that "enemies of all stripes still nurture strategic designs to topple our Cambodian revolution...." According to unofficial reports, casualties in the fighting totaled 2,500. Cambodian shelling into Vietnam was said to have forced the evacuation of border towns southwest of Saigon.

In the wake of the heavy border clashes between the two countries, Cambodia Dec. 31 severed diplomatic relations with Vietnam. A Foreign Ministry statement broadcast by Pnompenh radio said that the break would be "temporary" "until the aggressive forces of Vietnam withdraw from the sacred territory of Cambodia and until the friendly atmosphere between the two countries is restored." Cambodia charged that Vietnamese troops had been invading its territory since September 1977. The ministry demanded that Vietnamese diplomats in Pnompenh leave before Jan. 7, 1978. Hanoi earlier had withdrawn its ambassador from Pnompenh, an action described by the Cambodian Foreign Ministry as "unfriendly." Pnompenh also announced the suspension of the air link between the two countries.

Fighting along the Cambodian-Vietnamese borders continued through the month of January 1978. Hanoi radio charged Jan. 18 that Cambodian artillery had shelled targets in all eight Vietnamese provinces along the frontier since Jan. 9. According to the Vietnamese, Cambodian forces were still occupying a few areas in the southern border provinces of Kien Giang and An Giang and in Long An Province, which faced the Parrot's Beak, the scene of the heaviest fighting. In one action, the broadcast said, a Cambodian thrust into An Giang Jan. 11 killed or wounded 23 civilians and destroyed more than 200 houses. A Vietnamese counterattack, Hanoi radio claimed, forced the intruders back to Cambodia with a loss of more than 200 killed. In another clash, more than 300 Cambodian troops were killed Jan. 15 after they penetrated more than four kilometers (three miles) into Tay Ninh Province, Hanoi radio said.

Vietnam warned Cambodia Jan. 20 that its attacks were leaving Hanoi with no choice but to resort to "legitimate self-defense." The statement, in an editorial in the Vietnamese Communist Party newspaper *Nhan Dan*, was broadcast by Hanoi radio, which told of more Cambodian shelling of Vietnamese border villages. Cambodia and Vietnam Jan. 24 exchanged further charges of armed aggression. Hanoi radio said there were renewed Cambodian assaults against Vietnamese territory and that Cambodian troops were still holding seven areas in three Vietnamese border provinces. Pnompenh radio charged that Vietnam had carried out three incursions into Cambodian territory. Hanoi radio asserted Jan. 25 that Cambodian troops had driven into the southwestern Vietnamese district capital of Ha Tien. Vietnam Jan. 29 accused the Cambodians of shelling the hamlet of Long Chan Jan. 24-26, killing two civilians and wounding five. Further Cambodian attacks Jan. 27 on Tay Ninh Province killed and wounded a number of Vietnamese civilians, according to Hanoi.

Cambodia Jan. 30 boasted that its forces had "eliminated all of Vietnam's aggressive troops from Cambodian territory." This claim was followed by Pnompenh's accusation Feb. 1 of "continued acts of infiltration by the Vietnamese" into Cambodian territory. Hanoi radio countered the same day that Cambodian attacks against Vietnamese territory "have not ceased." According to a report from Bangkok Feb. 1, Vietnamese troops were moving in large numbers through southern Laos towards Cambodia. Cambodia Feb. 8 reported especially heavy fighting the previous day in the Mekong Delta in which it claimed that several hundred Vietnamese soldiers were killed. or wounded and 17 tanks were destroyed. The Vietnamese, the report added, were supported by MiG fighter planes and helicopters in their crossing of the Bassac River into Cambodian territory.

Call for Talks Rejected

Vietnamese Premier Pham Van Dong Jan. 5, 1978 had issued a call for talks with Cambodia "with a view to settling the border question." This invitation was followed, a month later, by another Vietnamese proposal that called for an immediate cease-fire. Hanoi's Feb. 5 proposal included, among other suggestions, a recommendaton that a demilitarized zone be established about four kilometers (three miles) on each side of the border; proposals for international supervision and guarantees of the truce agreement, and a call for an immediate meeting between the combatants. The accord, Vietnam said, should require both countries to respect each other's sovereignty, independence and territorial integrity. It also should commit them to renounce the use or threat of force and interference in each other's internal affairs. The Vietnamese statement called on Pnompenh to cease its propaganda, which it said created hatred between the two nations, in order to create a climate conducive to negotiations. It appealed to other nations and international organizations to make "positive contributions" to help bring about early peace talks between Vietnam and Cambodia. A copy of the statement was communicated Feb. 8 to U.N. Secretary General Kurt Waldheim, along with a request for U.N. support.

Cambodia spurned the Vietnamese bid for talks Feb. 8. In rejecting Hanoi's proposal, Pnompenh radio asserted Feb. 8 that "Although Vietnam's mouth calls for negotiations . . . , the truth is that Vietnam still continues to infiltrate repeatedly and commit barbarous aggression against Cambodia." Hanoi Feb. 9 accused Cambodia of responding to its peace proposal by launching new incursions into Vietnam. The broadcast did not give the location of the thrusts but said they were of "division strength."

China Takes Cambodia's Side

The Cambodian-Vietnamese border clashes drove Cambodia—or Kampuchea—farther into Chinese arms. This in turn strained China's relations with Vietnam.

Pol Pot, whose leadership of the Cambodian Communist Party had been disclosed for the first time in Pnompenh's official announcement of Sept. 25, 1977, arrived in Peking at the end of the month ostensibly to attend the Chinese National Day celebration Oct. 1 commemorating the establishment of the People's Republic of China. Pol Pot was greeted at Peking's airport Sept. 28 by Communist Party Chairman Hua Kuo-feng and other top Chinese leaders. A crowd of 100,000 cheered Pol Pot and his party as they were driven through the city's main square. His delegation included Ieng Sary, Cambodian deputy premier for foreign affairs. China's Hsinhua news agency identified Pol Pot as secretary of the Central Committee of the Cambodian Communist Party and as premier. It also named Ieng Sary as a member of the Standing Committee of the Central Committee. The news agency said that Pol Pot had been seen off at Pnompenh's airport that day by President Khieu Samphan and by Nuon Chea, identified by Hsinhua as chairman of the Standing Committee of the People's Representative Assembly.

At a banquet given in his honor later Sept. 28, Pol Pot said that conditions in his country were "excellent," and he made references to his country's recent border clashes with Vietnam and Thailand. Pol Pot boasted of the accomplishments of the Communist leadership since it had seized power in April 1975. "Social blemishes and the depraved culture . . . and other decadent phenomena in the age of imperialism, colonialism and the exploiting class have been basically abolished by the great mass movement in our country," he said. According to the premier, industry, agriculture and public health were flourishing, security in the country "was perfectly assured" and illiteracy had been reduced "by 80 to 90 percent." Pol Pot's glowing report of conditions in his country contrasted sharply with Cambodian refugee accounts of continued mass executions, forced migration of almost all urban residents to the countryside and Pnompenh's tyrannical rule.

Alluding to Cambodia's border clashes with Vietnam and Thailand, Pol Pot indicated that they concerned territories lost by his country in the 19th century. Because Cambodia had "lost much of its territories" during that period, its people "must defend our existing frontiers and see to it that they will never be lost," Pol Pot said.

Pol Pot's visit to China extended to Oct. 22 and was interrupted only by a short trip to Pyongyang, North Korea. In December, Peking sent to Pnompenh a high level delegation headed by Chen Yung-kuei, a member of the Politburo. At a banquet honoring him at Pnompenh, Chen asserted that China's relations with Cambodia were prompted by "pure friendship." The following month, another high level Peking delegation flew to Pnompenh. This delegation was headed by Teng Ying-chao, Chou En-lai's widow and a member of the

CCP Central Committee. Teng left Peking Jan. 18, 1978 and returned home Jan. 22. On her arrival in Peking at the end of the five day trip, Teng declared that her country regarded Cambodia as a victim of "Vietnamese aggression." This was reported to have been the first time that Peking directly criticized Hanoi over its frontier war with Cambodia.

Ethnic Chinese Exodus from Vietnam

Up to this time, the Chinese government had been following a cautious policy of avoiding an open rupture with Hanoi. It signed a trade agreement with Vietnam Jan. 10 for 1978. The accord provided for mutual supply of goods and payments. On the same day, the Chinese press published, for the first time, the Vietnamese version of the Cambodian-Vietnamese border conflict. The Vietnamese statement charged Cambodia with having "repeatedly intruded into Vietnamese territory since May 1975. The publication of this article followed the disclosure Jan. 9 by Nguyen Trong Vinh, Vietnamese ambassador to Peking, of a complaint he had made the previous week about China's press coverage of the conflict. Vinh said that he had "drawn attention" of the Chinese Foreign Ministry to his "dissatisfaction" with China's reporting of Hanoi's position in the combat. The ministry "rejected his views," Vinh added.

The spring of 1978 saw rapid deterioration of Sino-Vietnamese relations owing, largely, to the exodus from Vietnam of a large number of ethnic Chinese. The flight of the ethnic Chinese was attributed by the Vietnamese government to Peking's machination. At a press conference held in Havana, Cuba, Xuan Thuy, North Vietnamese Communist Party secretary, said July 29: "The Chinese side threatened Hoa [Chinese] people in Vietnam, saying that China was going to send troops to help Kampuchea fight Vietnam, that Soviet troops would also move in to support Vietnam, and that resident Chinese would be the first victims—so they must quickly return to China to avoid death and to join in national construction." Ethnic Chinese, some of whom had been settled in North Vietnam for generations crossed the borders into China's Kwangsi province in large numbers.

A new wave of ethnic Chinese refugees was reported in southern Vietnam in April. The Vietnamese government announced a drive Mar. 23 "to transform capitalist industry and to abolish trading activities of capitalists." The government was "placing trade under unified management,... [and] all trade business operations of bourgeois tradesmen are to be abolished," its statement said. While the government asserted that the new policy would be implemented "regardless of nationality," its campaign was in effect directed at the Chinese community in Saigon, which controlled most of the city's commerce. Of the 18 million persons in southern Vietnam, about one million were ethnic Chinese. Many of them had been forced to adopt Vietnamese citizenship during the regime of President Ngo Dinh Diem.

The head of the newly established Overseas Chinese Affairs Office in Pekng, Liao Cheng-chih, said May 1 that his country was concerned about the departure of the Chinese from Vietnam and that it was "closely following developments." He disclosed that "large numbers" of the refugees had "in recent days hastily returned to China." The Chinese embassy in Hanoi was said to regard the new Vietnamese economic laws as anti-Chinese and was angered when Vietnam rejected an embassy request to send a representative to Saigon to investigate.

Tension grew along the Chinese-Vietnamese frontier. Diplomatic sources in Hanoi reported May 1 that serious border clashes had broken out between Chinese and Vietnamese forces about April 20. Officials in Peking and Hanoi refused April 20 to confirm or deny the reports. However, the editor of the Vietnamese Communist Party newspaper *Nhan Dan* conceded in an interview published that day that there was tension along the frontier. According to an article in the *Far Eastern Economic Review*, Hoang Tung said that hostile feelings were generated by the massive deployment of Chinese troops along the Vietnamese border and by the beaming of Chinese propaganda by loudspeakers.

Most of the Chinese who had been expelled since early April 1978 came from the mountainous region in the northern half of the country. Other Chinese, from Ho Chi Minh City (formerly

Saigon), had fled by boat or plane to other places in Southeast
Asia after the government ordered the nationalization of busi-
nesses in the city. The move largely affected Chinese entrepre-
neurs. Hanoi was said to attribute the country's economic
decline since the end of the war in 1975 in large part to ethnic
Chinese domination of Vietnam's economy. Ethnic Chinese
controlled the rice trade, much of the black market, foreign
currency exchanges and the export-import business.

In a retaliatory move, the Chinese informed the Vietnamese
embassy in Peking May 12 that China would withdraw all 20 of
its aid projects and all of its 800 technical personnel from
Vietnam starting May 19. The Chinese said the personnel and
funds would be used to assist Chinese refugees from Vietnam
who had fled to southern China. Afterwards, Peking fired a
series of accusations at the Vietnamese for the alleged maltreat-
ment of ethnic Chinese. A May 24 statement charged that "the
massive expulsion of Chinese back to China is a purposeful
and planned line of action carried out by the Vietnamese
authorities." Peking announced May 27 that it wanted to send
ships to evacuate all "persecuted Chinese" from Vietnam. Peking claimed May 28 that 17,700 "victimized Chinese" had
crossed the border from Vietnam between May 21 and 26. This
brought the total of departures to nearly 90,000 persons since
the exodus started in 1977, with most of the refugees reaching
China since March, the statement said. The Vietnamese "are
continuing their persecution and expulsion of Chinese residents and the situation is deteriorating," the Hsinhua news
agency said.

The Vietnamese Foreign Ministry May 28 denied that the
Chinese in Vietnam had been mistreated. It insisted that a
majority of the people in Vietnam, including the ethnic Chinese, "had enthusiastically taken part" in the efforts to abolish
capitalism. The statement attributed the unrest to "a number of
bad elements" among the ethnic Chinese who had "deceived,
instigated, threatened and coerced" other Chinese into leaving
Vietnam for China. The ministry called for a meeting of China
and Vietnam to negotiate the dispute. The Vietnamese Foreign
Ministry May 29 repeated its appeal to China for negotiations
and suggested that the first meeting be held in Peking in early

June. The statement indicated Hanoi's willingness to consider China's May 27 proposal to send evacuation ships to Vietnam. The Vietnamese Communist Party newspaper *Nhan Dan* said May 29 that Hanoi wanted to preserve its friendship with China. At the same time, the journal denied that the country's ethnic Chinese were being persecuted. It said that the charges were false reports disseminated by the Chinese press and television. *Nhan Dan* pointed out that while China complained about the condition of the ethnic Chinese in Vietnam, it said "nothing about the plight of hundreds of thousands of Chinese working people and their families in Cambodia." This was a reference to the 500,000 ethnic Chinese in Cambodia from whom nothing had been heard since the cities had been emptied by the Communist rulers following their assumption of power in 1975.

China-Vietnam Ties Worsen

Hanoi June 5, 1978 granted China's request to send ships to evacuate ethnic Chinese from Vietnam. Two Chinese vessels sailed from Canton June 15 for Haiphong and Ho Chi Minh City. Neither ship, however, was permitted to land. The Vietnamese complained in a note to China June 19 that Peking had failed to provide the necessary information before the vessels could dock. This information included the capacity of the ships, the names of the crew members and plans for transporting the refugees. The Vietnamese also insisted that the transports could remain in harbor for three days only. This time limit would make it difficult if not impossible for the Chinese to complete their mission.

The Vietnamese Foreign Ministry charged June 22 that China had imposed six conditions of its own that would prevent the ships from landing. The ministry said it had rejected the demands in three days of negotiations with the Chinese. One demand called on Vietnam to accept Peking's description of the refugees as "Chinese residents who are victims of ostracism, persecution and expulsion by the Vietnamese authorities." Vietnam insisted on categorizing the refugees as "Vietnamese of Chinese descent" who merely "wish to leave Vietnam for China." China also wanted its embassy in Hanoi to be permitted to decide which of the refugees would be allowed to board the ships, and it insisted that no time limit be placed on the evacuation mission.

On the diplomatic front, China's deputy premier, Teng Hsiao-ping, announced June 5 and June 7 a reduction in China's economic assistance to Vietnam. He did not disclose the nature of the cut. His statement of June 7 intimated that some aid would continue. "The only thing wrong with our aid to Vietnam, if there is anything wrong with it at all, is that we have given Vietnam too much," Teng said. Cash assistance to Hanoi had totaled $18 billion, the deputy premier asserted, without specifying for what period. Teng accused Vietnam of "leaning toward the Soviet Union, which is an arch-enemy of China." He rejected Vietnamese offers for discussions to end the dispute, saying "there is still no foundation for such negotiations, either with Vietnam or the third country behind the conflict." Teng implied that the Soviet Union was the "third country."

Peking announced June 16, that it had recalled its ambassador from Hanoi, ostensibly for reasons of health. It was believed among diplomatic circles that the recall was directly related to the Chinese-Vietnamese conflict. Hanoi radio reported June 19 that Peking had ordered Vietnam to close its consulates in the Chinese cities of Canton, Nanning and Kunming. A Chinese diplomatic note published by Hanoi indicated that Peking had ordered the closures June 17 in retaliation for Vietnam's decision to delay establishment of a new Chinese consulate in Ho Chi Minh City. (Vietnam informed China June 17 that it could set up the consulate in October, but the two notes apparently crossed.)

The deteriorating Chinese-Vietnamese relations turned even worse June 23 when Vietnam became the 10th full member of the Council for Mutual Economic Assistance (Comecon), the economic association of the Soviet bloc. The admission of Vietnam was voted unanimously at the end of Comecon's annual summit meeting held June 27-29 in Bucharest, Rumania. Vietnam joined Cuba and Mongolia as the only non-European members of Comecon. Yugoslavia was an associate member; North Korea had observer status; Angola, Ethiopia and Laos sent observers to the meeting.

China reacted strongly against the latest pro-Soviet moves on the part of the Hanoi government. Peking announced July 3 that it was terminating all economic assistance to Vietnam. According to Hsinhua, the official Chinese news agency, a formal note handed to the Hanoi government cited Vietnam's alleged mistreatment of its ethnic Chinese. But diplomatic sources in Peking said they believed the principal reason for the move was China's displeasure with Vietnam's admission to Comecon. China was said to have based its decision also on its opposition to Vietnam's reputed plans to establish a federation in Indochina. Vietnam's preference for closer relations with the Soviet Union was cited as another reason. Hsinhua said the Vietnamese had been informed that Peking was discontinuing its aid program because of the "anti-China activities and ostracism of Chinese residents in Vietnam." All engineers and "other technical personnel" were being recalled, the Chinese note said.

A Vietnamese official July 4 discounted the impact of the Chinese action. Phan Hien, deputy minister for foreign affairs, said China had ended most of its assistance to his country in the past two years, and the final cut "did not affect us much." China's economic aid to Vietnam in the past 20 years was estimated at $10 billion, $3.24 billion of which had been provided in 1976. The 1977 figure was said to have been considerably less.

While the diplomatic situation was thus tense, a Hanoi broadcast July 11 alleged that four Chinese fighter planes had flown over Quang Minh and Cao Lang provinces, penetrating up to 19 miles (30 kilometers) into Vietnamese airspace. This allegation was dismissed by official Chinese sources July 12 as a "mere fabrication." At the same time, the Chinese Communist Party newspaper *Jenmin Jih Pao* accused Vietnam of attempting to control all of Southeast Asia in conjunction with the Soviet Union's expansionist activities. The newspaper said that the ouster of ethnic Chinese from Vietnam and Vietnamese attempts to disrupt relations between Peking and countries of Southeast Asia were part of a plot in which "the Soviet superpower with its own hegemonistic aims provides cover and support for the Vietnamese authorities' regional hegemonism."

Heavy Fighting Along Cambodian-Vietnamese Borders

There had been a lull in the fighting along Cambodian-Vietnamese borders between March and May 1978. The lull was broken with the resumption of fighting, which was reported from Western sources in Bangkok, Thailand May 17. Vietnam, according to these sources, had launched an offensive May 14 to counter Cambodian incursions. The heaviest clashes were reported in two Vietnamese-controlled areas on the Cambodian side of the border—the Parrot's Beak of Svay Rieng Province and the Mimot rubber plantation area in Kompong Chom Province. Fighting of similar intensity also was said to be raging in Cambodian-controlled areas in Vietnam's Tay Ninh and Kontum provinces.

Cambodia, for the first time, used tanks and other armored vehicles in the fighting between Tay Ninh Province, northwest of Ho Chi Minh City (Saigon), and Ha Tien, on the Gulf of Siam. This heavy equipment was believed to have been received from China in January at the Cambodian port of Kompong Som, in addition to long-range artillery.

Vietnamese forces inflicted heavy casualties on Cambodian troops in clashes inside Vietnam's An Giang and Tay Ninh provinces June 16-23, Hanoi radio reported June 27. Almost 160 troops were killed in two border battles June 20 and 23. A Cambodian regiment, according to the Vietnam News Agency, lost 35 men killed and wounded when it was intercepted after moving into An Giang Province June 16. In another action, Vietnamese troops wiped out one Cambodian battalion, caused heavy losses to two others and "captured a lot of arms and ammunition." Another Cambodian battallion was said to have been wiped out in the Ben Cau district of Tay Ninh, and many prisoners were captured, according to the agency.

Along with the escalation of fighting, both parties went through what had become by then a ritualistic exercise of waving an olive branch—public calls for peace talks. The Cambodian Foreign Ministry in May called on Hanoi to stop its attacks on Cambodia in order to create an atmosphere conducive to peace talks. In reply, Vietnam June 6 proposed a cease-fire. A Foreign Ministry note handed to Pnompenh said the truce and the establishment of a demilitarized zone along the frontier could be followed immediately by a conference of the two nations to settle their dispute.

But nothing came of these diplomatic overtures. Cambodian Deputy Premier Ieng Sary during his scheduled speech at the United Nations on disarmament charged June 9 that Vietnam had "relentlessly been harassing and provoking us along our frontiers." A Hanoi broadcast monitored in Tokyo June 27 said that the Vietnamese had wiped out two Cambodian battalions in fighting June 16-22, killing 160 of Pnompenh's soldiers. Both U.S. officials in Washington and Cambodia's ambassador to China, Pech Cheang, expressed doubt June 28 that Vietnam had launched a major drive. Pech Cheang had been quoted as saying the previous week that Cambodian border areas were coming under constant Vietnamese attack but that the Vietnamese had not occupied Cambodian territory in force since Jan. 6.

However, Western press reports from Bangkok, Thailand June 29 cited U.S. and Thai intelligence sources as saying that a force of 60,000 Vietnamese had mounted an offensive two weeks earlier and had pushed as much as 30 miles (48 kilometers) into Cambodia in some places. The drive, supported by artillery and air strikes, was said to have been coupled with Vietnamese broadcasts calling on Cambodians to overthrow their government because of its alleged massacre of its own people. While denying that the Vietnamese had mounted a large push, a Hanoi broadcast of June 29 said that in the previous few days Vietnamese soldiers had "killed several hundred" Cambodians who had "intruded into many districts" of Vietnam "and committed many crimes against the Vietnamese people." Tens of thousands of Vietnamese had been killed or wounded, Cambodia claimed July 3 in a summary of the fighting. A Pnompenh broadcast said that Vietnam was experiencing a shortage of supplies, that its troops were suffering from a lack of morale and that Vietnamese were fleeing the country to avoid being drafted into the armed forces to fight against Cambodia.

Amidst the deepening confusion on the military front, Pnompenh took to charging foreign powers with conspiracies to overthrow its goverment. Cambodian Deputy Premier Ieng Sary, during a stop in Tokyo June 13, 1978, accused the United States and Vietnam of having been involved in such plots. "There was an attempt," he said, "to topple our government in September 1975 as well as in 1976 and 1977." A Central Intelligence Agency (CIA) spokesman in Washington called Ieng's charges "preposterous." The Cambodian government renewed the accusation June 25, saying that it had crushed an attempt by Vietnam in May to overthrow the Cambodian government. Pnompenh radio accused Hanoi of "joining with its accomplices and collaborating" with the U.S. CIA in trying to carry out the coup. An Information Ministry spokesman said June 24 that six members of the Central Committee of Vietnam's ruling Communist Party had mapped plans for the uprising after what he termed Vietnam's setbacks in its border war against Cambodia. Since February, the six committee members and others had met secretly with Vietnamese officers in eastern Cambodia to organize the overthrow of the Pnompenh regime, the spokesman said.

The fighting continued, with both sides claiming victory. U.S. intelligence analysts in Washington reported Aug. 1 that Vietnam was carying out heavy air strikes in support of its troops inside Cambodia. The air strikes, in progress since mid-June, were concentrated largely in an area opposite Vietnam's Tay Ninh Province, scene of stiff Cambodian resistance, the report said. The Vietnamese pilots were assumed to be flying U.S.-built planes captured in the Indochina war. Western diplomatic sources in Bangkok, Thailand said July 31 that the hostilities of the previous two weeks had been the most intense that had taken place for some months. The fighting was said to be fiercest in the region north of the Parrot's Beak, Cambodian territory that jutted into southern Vietnam. A Pnompenh radio report July 31 said that at least 1,200 Vietnamese troops had been killed and 2,500 wounded in the fighting in July. A Vietnamese news agency report the previous day said that Hanoi's forces had put several Cambodian battalions "out of action" in clashes in the past week.

Refugee Talks Fail

The two Chinese vessels sent to Vietnam to evacuate ethnic Chinese had been anchored off Vietnamese shores since June 19, 1978. Meanwhile, Chinese and Vietnamese officials in Hanoi conducted 17 meetings but were unable to break the deadlock over procedures and over defining who was to be evacuated. In an effort to break the impasse, the Chinese government July 19 sent to the Vietnamese government a note proposing higher level talks in Peking—between deputy foreign ministers of both nations. The Chinese note suggested that once deputy foreign ministers meet, "the talks between the Chinese embassy [in Hanoi] and the Vietnamese department concerned with the question of transporting victimized Chinese nationals can adjourn for the time being." Peking called for an "overall settlement of the question of the Chinese nationals residing in Vietnam." This was in contrast to China's May 29 note to Vietnam, which had called for wider discussions that would consider Peking's decision to send ships to Vietnam to evacuate the ethnic Chinese, as well as other bilateral problems.

Vietnam accepted July 23 China's invitation. But even before the talks started, Peking and Hanoi traded charges over the refugee problem. Among the major developments were the following:

■ Vietnam charged July 20 that about 700 ethnic Chinese in Vietnam were prevented from crossing a bridge into China. Chinese border guards in Cao Lang Province had barred their entry, according to the statement.

■ Peking had protested to Hanoi that Vietnam was continuing to "drive to border areas and harass those victimized Chinese nationals who had not gone through the formalities to return to China," the Hsinhua news agency reported July 29. Vietnam in turn accused the Chinese embassy in Hanoi of rejecting requests for entry visas from ethnic Chinese who had returned from the Chinese-Vietnamese frontier to get them.

■ Vietnam called on China July 31 to take in more than 4,000 ethnic Chinese camped at the border. Hanoi said that the refugees were short of food and water and that 400 of them were ill.

■ Vietnam said Aug. 2 that China had instigated about
2,000 ethnic Chinese to stampede across the border into
China's Kwangsi Province Aug. 1. The refugees were forced to
return to the Vietnamese side of the frontier the following day,
according to a Hanoi broadcast Aug. 4. Vietnam's Aug. 2
statement said that China had encouraged the ethnic Chinese
to flee "to find a pretext for accusing the Vietnamese of expelling victimized Chinese and looting their property." A Peking
countercharge said Vietnam had driven the Chinese refugees
across the border.

The talks opened in Peking Aug. 8 and resumed in Hanoi
Aug. 15. The Chinese delegation was led by Deputy Foreign
Minister Chung Hsi-tung, and the Vietnamese delegation by
Deputy Foreign Minister Hoang Bich Son. At the opening
meeting, which was closed to the public, Chung was said to
have told the Vietnamese that Vietnam had violated a 1955
Chinese-Vietnamese agreement on the status of the ethnic
Chinese and had been "ostracizing, persecuting and expelling"
them. According to Hsinhua, Hoang Bich Son rejected the
Chinese contention, denying that Hanoi "had changed its previous position on the question of Chinese residents in Vietnam."

Even as talks were under way, repeated border incidents
further strained Chinese-Vietnamese relations. The Vietnamese news agency charged that more than 20 persons were
injured Aug. 8 in a Chinese-provoked attack on Vietnamese
border guards that forced or caused nearly 1,000 ethnic Chinese refugees to flee into China. China replied that Vietnamese
guards had initiated the assault, injuring 14 person and forcing
more than 700 ethnic Chinese to flee to the Chinese side.
Hsinhua said Aug. 21 that 21 Chinese refugees were forced to
cross the Peilun River into China Aug. 12, not far from a
regular border crossing. This pointed up Vietnam's continuing
campaign "to drive victimized Chinese into China through
rivers or other bypasses instead of Chinese border passes," the
Chinese news agency asserted.

In another incident Aug. 12, Vietnamese security forces used
tear gas to eject 120 ethnic Chinese from a hotel in Hanoi after

they rioted in the building, a Vietnamese official said Aug. 20. The Chinese, who had been put up in the hotel Aug. 10, demonstrated after they were told they could not leave for China because the Chinese embassy had failed to provide them with exit visas. About 100 others in the hotel whose papers were in order had been repatriated to China.

Another skirmish occurred Aug. 25, with at least 400 Vietnamese troops occupying Chinese territory in the vicinity of Friendship Pass, the frontier crossing linking Vietnam and China's Kwangsi province, Peking charged Aug. 28. According to the Chinese, the incident started when hundreds of Vietnamese soldiers and police attacked an ethnic Chinese refugee camp on the Vietnamese side of the border, driving more than 2,000 of the refugees into China. After the attack, a force of Vietnamese soldiers assaulted Bonien Hill on the China side, occupied the area, dug trenches and laid barbed wire. Peking further charged that the Vietnamese soldiers had also taken over hills on both sides of the Chinese border village of Nung Hua and had been responsible for "provocations" Aug. 26. Hsinhua indicated that seven refugees were killed. According to Hanoi's version of the incident, hundreds of Chinese police and soldiers in civilian clothes had joined "hooligans" among the refugees in an attack on Vietnamese border officials at the Vietnamese village of Dong Dang. Two of the officials were killed and several others were wounded, the statement said.

The Chinese delegation was recalled to Peking for consultation in the latter part of August. When it returned to Hanoi and resumed negotiations Sept. 7, the atmosphere had become tense with a new outburst of charges and countercharges of military provocations that had preceded the resumption of the talks. The Vietnamese Foreign Ministry had accused China Sept. 4 of "acts of provocation, troublemaking and encroachment upon Vietnam's territorial sovereignty, threatening her security." It said that on three occasions in August, Peking had sent "hundreds of Chinese fishing boats into Vietnamese territorial waters," interfering with the normal activities of Vietnamese fishermen. The Chinese were accused of sending fighter planes along the frontier and of violating airspace over Vietnam's Quang Ninh and Coalang provinces.

China's Hsinhua news agency accused Vietnam Sept. 4 of having "time and again sent armed military men and police to steal into Chinese territory in the vicinity of the Friendship Pass to try to abduct Chinese borderland inhabitants." China lodged a protest with Hanoi Sept. 5, charging that the Vietnamese had blocked a key railway link on the Chinese-Vietnamese border Aug. 30. The statement said the Vietnamese had pushed a railway car onto a bridge at the Friendship Pass crossing and surrounded it with barbed wire. The pass had been used by ethnic Chinese refugees from Vietnam to cross into China.

The talks made no headway. Finally, the negotiations were broken off by Peking Sept. 26, following the charge by Hanoi Sept. 25 that China was preparing war against Vietnam. A Hanoi broadcast of that date said that China had massed its armed forces for an invasion of northern Vietnam on "two fronts." Although Hanoi radio did not identify the areas, Western military sources in Singapore said tensions had been building up on the frontiers of China's Yunnan and Kwangsi provinces. The broadcast said that "whole divisions of infantry equipped with thousands of artillery pieces, hundreds of fighter planes are poised in two Chinese military regions bordering Vietnam." The statement charged that "various types of ships are carrying out acts of provocation in Vietnam."

Before leaving Hanoi, Chinese Deputy Foreign Minister Chung Hsi-tung said that Vietnam had been "using the talks to camouflage violence and using violence to undermine the talks." The head of the Chinese delegation further charged that the "deterioration of the talks to such an extent in less than two months' time is correlated to the escalation of the anti-Chinese activities of the Vietnamese authorities over the same period." Chung accused Vietnam of "expelling, abducting, arresting and even killing Chinese nationals at border passes" and in Hanoi.

Vietnam claimed that its delegation had insisted that the talks continue. "In the face of such a good-willed attitude on our side," it was "beyond everyone's understanding" for China to accuse Hanoi of sabotaging the meetings, the statement said. Vietnamese delegate Hoang Bich Son charged that China had made "completely unrealistic points" at the discussions and had leveled groundless accusations as a pretext for breaking off the conference. At the latest session, Vietnam had suggested that the conferees first take up the question of "Chinese residents who fled Cambodia for refuge in Vietnam." While there was no doubt about the nationality of those refugees, there was disagreement over whether most ethnic Chinese in Vietnam were Chinese citizens or had adopted Vietnamese nationality, Son argued. Son also proposed that China and Vietnam consider two other categories: Chinese residents who carried Hong Kong and Taiwan identity cards and the Hoa people, ethnic Chinese of both north and south Vietnam.

Chinese delegate Chung claimed that Hanoi had taken the position at the talks that all the ethnic Chinese in Vietnam had already become Vietnamese citizens, "except a few who hold identity cards issued in Taiwan and Hong Kong." Chung had charged at the Sept. 19 session of the Hanoi talks that Vietnam had launched a war of aggression against Cambodia "to subvert its revolutionary regime." He also said the Vietnamese had stationed troops in Laos "in an attempt to control the whole of Indochina and then go on to expand to Southeast Asia."

Awakening to Human Rights

Publication of Rights Abuses

The purge of the "Gang of Four" rekindled interest in the question of human rights in the People's Republic of China. The interest was genuine enough. For during the Cultural Revolution a large number of officials had been hounded out of office by the Red Guards and made to endure public humiliation and private hardships. These officials were now being rehabilitated. To them, civil rights were not merely an abstract legal concept but something to which they could relate through bitter personal experience. Beyond that, the question of human rights provided a political issue that served the new leadership well. It could be used to discredit the "Gang of Four" and rally the public behind the new government program of modernization.

Once securely installed, the new regime began publicizing the abuses of human rights that had occurred previously. The Chinese Communist Party newspaper *Jenmin Jih Pao* Nov. 28, 1977 published an official statement by the Ministry of Public Security critical of the national police. And Peking continued to publicize cases of human rights violations in China, with an indication that it would correct these abuses, the *New York Times* reported Feb. 28, 1978. In one case, *Jenmin Jih Pao* published a letter written by the wife of an official who said she was unable to get a job after the investigation of her husband on undisclosed charges. She also complained that her daughter had trouble getting into the Young Communist League and that her son was barred from enlisting in the army. The government official who received the woman's letter replied that "neither family origin nor parental behavior should be used as the sole criterion" in judging people.

In one of the worst cases of rights abuse, the Hsinhua news agency reported, "hundreds of people" in the Shanghai branch of the Academy of Sciences were falsely accused during the Cultural Revolution of being Chinese Nationalist agents. Their families were still being discriminated against, Hsinhua said.

Strengthening the Socialist Legal System

The publication of rights abuses presaged the constitutional revision at the Fifth National People's Congress, which took place Feb. 26-March 5, 1978. The new constitution, which replaced the constitution of 1975, underscored the concern of the new leadership for the protection of civil rights—or at least for preventing some of the more gross violations. In the chapter dealing with the fundamental rights and duties of citizens, the 1975 constitution had only four articles. By comparison, the corresponding section of the new constitution contained sixteen articles, twelve of which pertained to citizens' rights.

Among the rights provided for under the new constitution were: freedom of speech, of correspondence, of the press, of association, of procession, and of demonstration and the freedom to strike. These rights were, on paper, hardly distinguishable from those found in Western democracies. However, their actual meaning should be understood within the framework of the PRC's political structure, which was based on Marxist-Leninist orthodoxy and Mao Tse-tung's thought. Such freedoms were to be enjoyed by the "people," not by their enemies. In a commentary on the new constitution, *Jenmin Jih Pao* May 3 reiterated the CCP (Chinese Communist Party) position: "Towards the enemy there is dictatorship."

"The new constitution," the *Jenmin Jih Pao* article declared, "lays it down clearly that landlords, kulaks, and reactionary capitalists, if not reformed, are deprived of political rights; that traitors, counter-revolutionary elements and other bad elements are punished; and in accordance with the present reality of class struggle in our country, it adds that new-born bourgeois elements also are punished." The new-born bourgeois elements were defined as "those who resist the socialist revolution, endanger socialist construction, seriously damage socialist common property, embezzle society's wealth or commit criminal acts."

This list of excluded classes—excluded from the enjoyment of constitutional freedoms—was long indeed. But the new constitution showed a marked broadening of freedoms for the "people," compared with what was available under the old constitution; it also showed an attempt to raise legal barriers against the arbitrary and capricious use of power. This was particularly the case with respect to intellectual activities in science and technology: "Citizens have the freedom to engage in scientific research, literary and artistic creation and other cultural activities." Previously, such intellectual and cultural activities were to be subject to "all-round dictatorship" of the proletariat. Under the new constitution, this requirement of political control was replaced by a more general statement: "The state upholds the leading position of Marxism-Leninism-Mao Tse-tung Thought in all spheres of ideology and culture."

The new constitution curtailed the powers of the state security organ. Under the old constitution, a person could be arrested legally either by decision of a people's court or "with the sanction of a public security organ." The new constitution removed the power to "sanction" arrests from a public security organ and gave it to a "people's procurate." To arrest a person, a public security organ would be required to obtain a warrant from a people's procurate or act under the order of a people's court. In all cases, the accused would be heard "in public" and enjoy the right of defense.

Yeh Chien-ying, who introduced the new constitution at the National People's Congress March 1, stressed the need for a nationwide campaign to educate the masses about their new constitutional rights: "We should see to it that all who support socialism feel that their freedom of person, democratic rights and legitimate interests as prescribed by the constitution are solidly assured." Premier Hua Kuo-feng, in his earlier speech before the Congress Feb. 26, had likewise emphasized the rule of law. "It is essential," Hua said, "to strengthen 'the Socialist Legal System' if we are to bring great order into being across the land."

Jenmin Jih Pao picked up the theme of "the Socialist Legal System." In its March 16 issue, the newspaper featured an article by Han Yu-tung, 70-year-old woman lawyer and vice president of the Chinese Academy of Social Sciences. Han argued that there was an urgent need for enacting civil and criminal codes as well as establishing machineries for implementing them. "There are people who worry and dare not touch the problem of making, implementing and observing laws; they dare not study the present situation, courageously studying and solving the questions."

'Gang of Four' Victims Rehabilitated

Those who stood to gain most directly from the new thrust toward the Socialist Legal System were the victims of the ideological crusade under the aegis of the "Gang of Four." The rehabilitation of ousted officials proceeded at the national and local levels in tune with the new policy. *Jenmin Jih Pao* reported March 13 that more than 10,000 Shanghai purge victims of the "Gang of Four" had been rehabilitated, some posthumously. They included cadres, workers, intellectuals and artists. The article said that the authorities had cleared the victims by canceling wrong verdicts, adjusting improper work assignments and assisting "children of persecuted parents who met discrimination."

The "Gang of Four" was further linked with a series of "astounding miscarriages of justice" in Anhwei Province, according to a provincial broadcast April 11. The statement said that a fire at a steel plant in 1969 had been used as a pretext to accuse 1,000 persons of arson, many of whom were killed or injured "as a result of being persecuted," the broadcast reported.

As the spring of 1978 moved on, the rehabilitation picked up tempo. Chinese sources in Hong Kong reported June 5 that Peking had recently released 110,000 persons who had been detained since the start of an "anti-rightist" campaign in 1957. The report, quoting accounts from China's provinces, also indicated that a rehabilitation program was under way for many lower-level Communist Party officials, intellectuals and other citizens purged in the Cultural Revolution in the 1960s or during the 1975-76 period when the so-called radicals held sway.

The drive to reinstate these people was said to have been pressed personally by Deputy Premier Teng Hsiao-ping. The campaign was believed connected with the government's desire to help regain its popular prestige and to make better use of skilled manpower in its program to modernize the country. The rehabilitation program was said to have encountered some resistance, especially the effort to find new jobs for those who had been ousted. It was feared that employees in the same place of business might have numerous scores to settle with each other. Some officials who were responsible for the purges were said to be afraid they might lose face or their jobs. Others were reported to be concerned that the government might scrap the new program as it had others in the past.

An Anhwei Province broadcast referred to these problems in charging that some "leading comrades have put fear before anything else. Some leadership personnel who handle cases have been selfish and have worried about their own personal gain and loss." Another broadcast, from Kweichow Province, noted that "some leading comrades fear that verdicts on a movement of one year may be reversed three years later and dare not boldly lead the movement."

The rehabilitation program uncoverd for the first time incidents of torture that were coupled with the purges. The Hsinhua news agency reported that in Shanghai "tens of thousands" of people had been "cruelly tortured or persecuted" by radicals in their drive to consolidate their control over the city. In another incident, Hsinhua said, more than 1,000 people in the Ministry of Culture in Peking had been purged, imprisoned or tortured to exact confessions. Some of the victims "became disabled, went insane or died," and their "families were totally ruined" or missing, Hsinhua said.

One of the prominent figures who were posthumously rehabilitated was Tsao Ti-chiu, former mayor of Shanghai. Tsao had been purged during the Cultural Revolution in December 1967. *Jenmin Jih Pao* reported June 28, 1978 that he had been posthumously rehabilitated June 23. Tsao, who died in Shanghai in March 1976, had been mayor from 1965 until his dismissal two years later. He was accused of being an "agent" of former head of state Liu Shao-chi. Tsao's ashes were brought to Peking June 28 to be placed in a cemetery containing the remains of China's revolutionary heroes. The rehabilitation ceremonies were held in Shanghai after Tsao's case was

reexamined on orders of the Communist Party's Central Committee. *Jenmin Jih Pao* said Tsao had been "slandered for a
long time" and was "savagely persecuted mentally and physically" by the now-purged "Gang of Four and their lackeys."
The newspaper singled out the leader of the group, Chiang
Ching. Chang Chun-chiao, who was later to become a member
of the "Gang of Four," became mayor of Shanghai on Tsao's
dismissal from the post.

Thaw Induced by Drive for Modernization

The spring of 1978 saw a continuing thaw in the internal
policies of the PRC (People's Republic of China). Sources
inside the People's Republic gave accounts of renewed religious activity in that country; the accounts were reported
March 10 in the *New York Times*.

For the first time since the Cultural Revolution, more than a
decade previously, some small Chinese groups had worshipped
Feb. 26 at Sunday church services. The only prior exceptions
for church worship had been on special occasions such as
Christmas. The account cited a group of Chinese Roman
Catholics that had attended a regular service in Peking (the
Catholic cathedral there had continued to function for foreign-
ers) and another group that had attended a Protestant service
in Nanking. Also reported was a visit by a diplomat from a
Buddhist country to a Buddhist pagoda in Peking. He was
received by the abbot. This was the first time in many years that
such a visit had been arranged. During the same week, the
Chinese People's Political Consultative Conference convened.
(The conference was established to represent nonparty groups.)
A number of Roman Catholic, Protestant and Buddhist leaders appeared at the meeting for the first time since the early
1960s. No official statement was issued by the government to
indicate how extensive toleration of religious observances
would be in the future.

In no small measure impetus toward the protection of
human rights emerged from the drive for modernization of
industry, agriculture, national defense and science and technology ("the four modernizations"). The two, in fact, proceeded
hand in hand.

China announced the launching of an eight-year major drive to improve its scientific and technological development during a national science conference held in Peking March 18, 1978. The plan was detailed in a speech by Politburo member Fang Yi. Fang, who was minister in charge of the State Scientific & Technological Commission, said in his address, made public May 28, that China was "now lagging 15 to 20 years behind in many branches and still more in some others." He urged a speedup of scientific development as the only way for China to "catch up with or surpass the capitalist countries." At the conclusion of the eight-year program, it was hoped that China "will approach or reach advanced world levels of the 1970s in a number of important branches of science and technology," Fang said. This would narrow the gap to about 10 years, "laying the foundation for catching up with or surpassing advanced world levels in all branches in the following 15 years," Fang added.

The government had drawn up a draft plan of 108 projects that would concentrate on these principal fields: agriculture, energy, coal mining, materials reach, laser development, space technology, high-energy physics and genetic engineering. Among the improvements sought were the further mechanization of agriculture and coal mining and the development of 10 more oilfields.

In July 1978, Hua Kuo-feng, the Chinese Communist Party chairman, declared that China must "learn from the advanced experience of other countries" to expand its own economy and international trade. Hua made the remark July 7 in a speech at a national conference on finance and trade in Peking. In his address, Hua acknowledged deficiencies in China's economy and trade practices. Although China had made great progress, "there isn't the least reason for complacency," Hua warned. He cited improvements in China's economy for the January-June 1978 period. According to preliminary statistics released by Hua, industrial production had increased 24% over the equivalent six-month period of 1977. Steel output was up 67%, petroleum up 11%, coal 19% and electricity up 17%. "Output of 16 major products of light industry, including cotton yarn, paper and sugar, increased by wide margins," the party chairman added. At the same time, Hua noted that some Chinese

officials were not aware of their country's backwardness or of
what had been going on abroad. Among the country's economic shortcomings he cited were "low productivity, poor
quality of products, high production costs, low profits and
slow turnover of funds. A number of enterprises are still running at a loss."

Hua's speech underscored Peking's new policy of adopting
from the West the modern techniques of industrial and financial management. According to a July 6 report, Peking had
authorized managers of the Bank of China and its 12 sister
banks in Hong Kong to practice "capitalist methods" as long as
they were "confident of making a profit." In addition to the
general guideline, the banks were specifically given authority
to buy and sell stocks and bonds, gold, silver and other com-
modities, foreign currencies and real estate. Despite Peking's
instructions, it was said then that none of the Chinese banks in
Hong Kong apparently had yet instituted the new policy. One
source was quoted as saying that "everyone is afraid of taking
risks. There isn't any guarantee that you can make a profit in
every trading activity, and if you suffer a loss you may be held
responsible."

The Bank of China in Hong Kong was the principal foreign-
exchange arm of the Peking government. Along with its 12
affiliates, the bank operated more than 130 branch offices in
the British colony. It was second only to Hongkong &
Shanghai Banking Corp., which had more than 150 branches
in Hong Kong. China's banks controlled about one-third of
Hong Kong's $12.5 billion in total bank deposits.

The directive, announced the previous week, represented a
major reversal of the "socialist character" of China's banking
policies. It also reflected the continued trend of China's new
pragmatic approach toward political and economic practices
in the wake of the death of Chairman Mao Tse-tung and the
overthrow of the radical "Gang of Four." The new practical
policies that were being followed included the elimination of
revolutionary committees to operate factories; new methods to
encourage greater industrial production, efficiency and special-
ization, and granting permission to students to go directly into
university after graduating from middle school, without going

through the previously required two-year work period in a factory or on a farm.

Keeping in steps with this trend, the Chinese government abolished the long-standing directive prohibiting contacts between Chinese citizens and foreigners residing in Peking. The order lifting the ban, which was made public Sept. 9, 1978, reportedly had been issued earlier in the week by Deputy Premier Teng Hsiao-ping. The order appeared to be in accord with what was described as Teng's strongly-held belief that China must break out of its self-imposed isolation if it was to catch up with the industrialized nations of the world. Foreign residents in Peking were said to have noticed earlier in the year a slackening of police surveillance of meetings between Chinese citizens and outsiders. All foreigners in Peking lived in walled compounds and were completely cut off from all but the most superficial contacts with Chinese people around them. Until the restrictions were lifted, army troops had controlled access to the compounds, permitting entry only to domestic servants, workers and the few Chinese Foreign Ministry officials authorized to visit foreigners at their homes.

Modernization through emulation of the West was a major theme of Chairman Hua's National Day speech Oct. 1. Hua said that China's "national economy is embarking on a path of sustained rapid advance. There has emerged an excellent situation of stability, unity, greater drive and higher efficiency." At the same time, Hua stressed the need to "further emancipate our minds.... We must give full play to the superiority of our socialist system... and put to use the advanced experience of foreign countries."

Criticism of Mao Catches Fire

The new trend did not replace the old system. In charting the course for modernization, the new leadership in Peking took care not to destroy the legendary stature of the deceased Chairman Mao Tse-tung. But it was difficult to contain the impact of the new policy; the repudiation of the past practices was bound to cast aspersions on Chairman Mao.

In 1978, in an article marking the 57th anniversary of the founding of the Chinese Communist Party, the two principal publications—*Jenmin Jih Pao* and the party theoretical journal *Hung Chi*—published an indirect criticism of Mao saying that the late chairman had failed to promote democracy in the party. Both journals published editorials urging more democracy. *Jenmin Jih Pao* attributed the lack of freedom in the party to the rise in power of Lin Piao, the late defense minister, and the "Gang of Four" purged radicals. The newspaper praised Mao's successor, Chairman Hua Kuo-feng, for having "opened broad channels for the airing of views." It said that since Hua's assumption of the chairmanship, "the vitality of democracy has been apparent." The two editorials affirmed the party's "democratic centralism." Under this system democracy and central leadership existed side by side.

The Hsinhua news agency published a speech delivered by Mao in January 1962 in which he admitted to "shortcomings and mistakes." Mao was quoted as having conceded that except for his knowledge of agriculture, "I still don't know much" about other aspects of the country's economy, such as industry and commerce." The need to reevaluate Mao's precepts previously had been urged by Deputy Premier Teng Hsiao-ping, it was reported June 3, 1978. Speaking at a conference of army political commisars, Teng said that Mao's ideas should not be interpreted literally. "We must integrate them with reality, analyze and study actual conditions and solve practical problems," he said. "If we just copied past documents word for word, we wouldn't be solving any problem, let alone solving any problem correctly," Teng declared.

Then, in November, a more direct criticism of Mao surfaced by implicating him with the discredited "Gang of Four." The criticism was contained in a wall poster that appeared in Peking Nov. 14. The poster, which was signed by workers at a garage, apparently received tacit government approval since no attempt was made to remove it. The poster ostensibly dealt with a new play related to the 1976 riots in Peking's Tien An Men Square, which led to the temporary downfall of Deputy Premier Teng. The poster said: "Chairman Mao, because his thinking was metaphysical thinking during his old age and for all kinds of other reasons, supported the "Gang of Four" in raising their hands to strike down" Teng. After the Peking riots, the statement continued, the "Gang of Four" had used "Mao's mistaken judgment about class struggle and used the situation to launch an all-out offensive against China's revolutionary cause."

The Peking poster attacking Mao was part of a growing campaign in 1978 to downgrade the late chairman. Further evidence of this was contained in a Nov. 15 Peking newspaper article, which called a November 1965 essay endorsed by Mao to launch the Cultural Revolution counter-revolutionary. The essay, written by Yao Wen-yuan, a member of the "Gang of Four," was "a reactionary signal to practice fascist dictatorship," the article said. *Jenmin Jih Pao* said Nov. 16 that all Communist Party officials who had been mistakenly purged before, during and after the Cultural Revolution would be fully rehabilitated by the middle of 1979. "It must be admitted some innocent people were wrongly charged," the journal said.

The criticism of Mao inevitably affected his handpicked successor. Wall posters indirectly critical of Mao and of the current chairman, Hua Kuo-feng, appeared in Peking and other major Chinese cities starting Nov. 20. The posters, which also called for more democracy in the country, were part of a new, intense political campaign marked by the unusual staging of outdoor rallies in which participants demanded civil liberties and respect for human rights. In addition to the posters and rallies, articles appeared attacking the Cultural Revolution of the 1960s as a "counterrevolutionary fascist dictatorship" and revealing that the authors of several famous wall posters in the Cultural Revolution had been arrested and punished as counterrevolutionaries.

Deputy Premier Teng Hsiao-ping gave qualified approval to the latest poster campaign, saying: "If the masses feel some anger, we must let them express it." However, he cautioned the protesters that "some utterances are not in the interest of stability and unity. We have to explain matters clearly to the masses and know how to lead."

Two wall posters appearing in Peking Nov. 20 called for an investigation of the arrests of demonstrators at the rally in Tien

An Men Square April 5, 1976, staged ostensibly in memory of the recently deceased Premier Chou En-lai. The statement said "those responsible for the suppression and cover-up could be brought to justice." This raised questions about the status of Chairman Hua. Two days after the Peking demonstration, Teng, at Mao's behest, had been purged as deputy premier, and Hua was named premier as well as first deputy chairman of the Communist Party. A further reference to the Tien An Men Square incident Nov. 23 accused Mao of helping put down the demonstration and charged that he was behind Teng's ouster. The placard also directly linked Mao to the activities of two of China's most disgraced leaders, Mao's wife, Chiang Ching, and former Defense Minister Lin Piao.

Two Communist leaders purged by Mao were praised on a poster put up in Peking Nov. 24. The placard said that Peng Teh-huai, ousted as defense minister in 1959, had "merits ... greater than his mistakes." Peng had been dropped after criticizing Mao's Great Leap Forward, a program designed to increased production primarily with small-scale works. The other purged leader praised by the poster was Tao Chu, who had been removed in 1968 as deputy premier in a widespread shakeup of the government. The poster also attacked two former heads of the state security apparatus who were close to Mao. They were Kang Sheng, long-time head of the intelligence and secret police, who died in 1975, and Hsieh Fu-chih, head of the Public Security Ministry during much of the Cultural Revolution in the 1960s.

Two posters displayed in Peking Nov. 25 were critical of the backwardness of China and of the way Hua was appointed premier in 1976. One of the placards, which was pasted up on a fence facing Mao's mausoleum, said: "America is a capitalist country and is the most developed in the world. The United States is only 200 years old, but it has developed because [unlike China] it has no idols or superstitions." The second poster questioned the two Mao-proposed resolutions dismissing Teng and appointing Hua as his successor. It stated: "The two resolutions are not products of Marxism but the willful products of futile, fascist dictatorship. They went against democracy and the legal system." According to China's Constitution, the premier must be appointed by the National People's Congress, the legislature, the poster pointed out.

In one of several outdoor rallies staged in Peking, several thousand persons marched Nov. 27 through the downtown area, chanting, "Chinese democracy! Long live democracy!" Following the march, U.S. correspondent Robert Novak, who had interviewed Teng earlier in the day, sent word to a waiting crowd through another journalist about the remarks made to him by the deputy premier. Novak said Teng had told him that the posters were "a good thing" but that some of them were not correct, especially those criticizing Mao. A rally in the capital Nov. 28 was attended by about 10,000 Chinese, who cheered speakers demanding democracy and human rights.

Presumably fearing possible disturbances, the Chinese authorities Nov. 30 ordered a halt to the posting of placards criticizing Hua and to the demonstrations. Despite the directive, posters continued to appear through Dec. 10. A poster appearing in Peking, Dec. 3 called for the prosecution of the "Gang of Four." A poster appeared in Peking Dec. 10 calling on U.S. President Jimmy Carter "to pay attention to the state of human rights in China," but it was immediately torn down by a man who claimed that it was written by a Soviet agent. Signed by "The Human Rights Group," the placard was a copy of one pasted on a wall Dec. 7 that also had been removed.

A rally attended by 10,000 persons in Shanghai Dec. 10 expressed support for democracy and modernization, Western travelers reported in Hong Kong the following day. The travelers also said they had seen posters in major cities other than in Peking—Shanghai, Tientsin, Nanking, Wuhan, Chunking and Canton.

The Normalization of Relations With the U.S.

The Breakthrough

For nearly a decade since President Richard M. Nixon's 1972 visit to China, the establishment of normal diplomatic relations between Peking and Washington had been stalemated over the Taiwan issue. Both sides were interested in the normalization, but bringing it off required a diplomatic ingenuity that neither side had been able to muster. Peking stood adamantly on its demand that the United States break off its diplomatic relations with the Nationalist government on Taiwan and terminate the mutual defense pact as well. Given the premise, which the United States did not challenge, that there was only one China, Peking's position was unassailable. But accommodating it presented formidable difficulties for the United States, for the support of Chinese Nationalists was deeply encrusted in American politics.

Negotiations to circumvent the Taiwan issue began to accelerate following the visit to Peking in May 1978 of U.S. national security adviser Zbigniew Brzezinski. Brzezinski said at that time that President Jimmy Carter "desires friendly relations with a strong China." Privately he had told Deputy Premier Teng Hsiao-ping and Chairman Hua Kuo-feng that Leonard Woodcock, the head of the U.S. liaison office in Peking, was prepared to start serious talks. Those discussions began in earnest in July. The key issues throughout the meetings remained whether the U.S. could continue to sell arms to Taiwan after the normalization of ties with China. Chai Tse-min, head of the Chinese liaison office in Washington, met Sept. 19 with Carter, who was said to have made three points: the U.S. must continue its current commercial and cultural ties with Taiwan; the U.S. believed that the Chinese-Taiwan dispute must be resolved peacefully, and the U.S. should be permitted to continue to sell arms to Taiwan after the normalization of U.S.-Chinese relations.

The U.S. Nov. 4 sent to the Chinese a draft of a joint communique. Carter personally set Jan. 1, 1979 as the target date for establishing diplomatic relations. He was said to have reached this decision in October after the successful conclusion of the Camp David summit meeting with Israel and Egypt.

In mid-November the Chinese asked for clarification. On Nov. 25 Deputy Premier Teng said publicly that he hoped to visit Washington. This remark was regarded by the White House as a signal by the Chinese that they were anxious for an agreement. Early in December Woodcock was informed by the Chinese that Teng was prepared to see him, and on Dec. 4 the Chinese presented a draft of their own proposed joint com munique.

Brzezinski informed Chai Dec. 11 that an invitation was being extended to Teng to visit the U.S. The following day the White House received word of Teng's acceptance and also of Chinese approval of the U.S.' terms for the treaty. The U.S. informed China Dec. 7 of its insistence on continuing arms sales to Taiwan, a demand rejected by Peking. The following day both sides apparently agreed to leave this controversial question in abeyance; this presumed decision cleared the way for the final U.S.-Chinese agreement.

An agreement to normalize Washington-Peking ties was reached Dec. 14, 1978 following several months of secret nego-tiations. The accord was announced simultaneously by Presi-dent Carter Dec. 15 (Washington time) and by Chairman Hua Kuo-feng Dec. 16 (Peking time). In a dramatic and unexpected speech on national television, Carter read a U.S.-Chinese joint communique saying: the U.S. and China had agreed to estab-lish diplomatic relations, effective Jan. 1, 1979; Chinese Dep-uty Premier Teng Hsiao-ping was to visit the U.S. Jan. 29; and both sides were to exchange ambassadors and establish embas-sies March 1.

On the Taiwan issue, the joint communique said: "The Uni-ted States recognizes the government of the People's Republic of China as the sole legal government of China. Within this context the people of the United States will maintain cultural, commercial and other unofficial relations with the people of Taiwan."

In his speech, which followed the reading of the joint com-munique, Carter asserted that the normalization action was being taken not "for transient, tactical reasons" but for "acknowledgment of simple reality." In an official statement issued separately, the United States declared that it would terminate its diplomatic relations with Taiwan as of Jan. 1, 1979 and terminate the mutual defense pact with the Taiwan regime at the end of 1979. The President assured Taiwan that although the U.S. was cancelling its defense treaty with Taipei as of Dec. 31, 1979, the Administration would "maintain cultural, commercial and unofficial relations with the people of Taiwan." U.S.-Chinese diplomatic ties, he said, "will not jeopardize the well-being of the people of Taiwan." He expressed the hope that Taiwan's dispute with Peking would be resolved peacefully.

Carter said that the U.S. and China reaffirmed the principles contained in the 1972 Shanghai communique, drawn up at the conclusion of President Nixon's visit with the late Premier Chou En-lai. Both nations, Carter said, "emphasized once again" their desire "to reduce the danger of international military conflict. Neither should seek hegemony . . . in the Asia-Pacific region or in any other region of the world, and each is opposed to efforts by any other country or group of countries to establish such hegemony."

After his speech, Carter told newsmen that the agreement would open "a new vista of trade relations with the almost one billion people of China." He said that he felt "the security of Taiwan is adequately protected" under the accord.

An official Chinese statement issued Dec. 16, after Chairman Hua's reading of the joint communique, stressed the problem of Taiwan. It said that question "has now been resolved" with the U.S. "in the spirit of the Shanghai communique through their joint efforts." The statement added, "As for the way of bringing Taiwan back to the embrace of the motherland and reunifying the country, it is entirely China's internal affair." The U.S., however, took a different view. A U.S. State Department official Dec. 17 emphasized that the Carter Administration intended that "all existing agreements with Taiwan, commercial, cultural and others, will continue in effect except for termination of the defense treaty." The U.S. had about 60 formal agreements with Taiwan. Some of these accords had been reached with the Chinese Nationalists while they controlled the mainland of China before their defeat by the Communists in 1949. In addition to the defense and mutual security agreements, the accords concerned agricultural products, atomic energy, aviation, finance, trade and commerce and economic and technical cooperation.

Secretary of State Cyrus Vance said Dec. 17 that the U.S. did not expect China to use force to regain Taiwan, although China gave the U.S. no such pledge in their agreement to establish diplomatic relations. Appearing on NBC-TV's *Meet the Press* program, Vance said that, "as a practical matter," it would be pointless for China to invade Taiwan because Peking wanted improved relations with the U.S. and other nations. "It would be totally inconsistent for them to take action contrary to what we have indicated is of essential importance to us," the secretary added.

A U.S. Defense Department official had disclosed Dec. 16 that the U.S. had decided to continue to sell arms to Taiwan on a selective basis in order to keep its American-equipped forces in shape and to maintain stability in the region. The official's statement was coupled with a report of a Pentagon proposal, called "Consolidated Guidance 9," suggesting continued and even increased weapons sales to Taiwan to parallel a break in U.S. military and diplomatic relations with Nationalist China. The document was said to have been drawn up at the request of the White House to assess Taiwan's military needs after normalization of U.S. relations with Peking.

Carter's Announcement on U.S. Ties with China

Following is the text of President Carter's Dec. 15, 1978 TV speech announcing U.S. diplomatic relations with China:

Good evening. I would like to read a joint communique which is being simultaneously issued in Peking at this very moment by the leaders of the People's Republic of China:

"A Joint Communique on the Establishment of Diplomatic Relations Between the United States of America and the People's Republic of China, Jan. 1, 1979.

"The United States of America and the People's Republic of China have agreed to recognize each other and to establish diplomatic relations as of Jan. 1, 1979.

"The United States recognizes the government of the People's Republic of China as the sole legal government of China. Within this context the people of the United States will maintain cultural, commercial and other unofficial relations with the people of Taiwan.

"The United States of America and the People's Republic of China reaffirm the principles agreed on by the two sides in the Shanghai Communiqué of 1972 and emphasize once again that both sides wish to reduce the danger of international military conflict. Neither should seek hegemony—that is the dominance of one nation over the others—in the Asia-Pacific region or in any other region of the world and each is opposed to efforts by any other country or group of countries to establish such hegemony.

"Neither is prepared to negotiate on behalf of any third party or to enter into agreements or understandings with the other directed at other states.

"The government of the United States of America acknowledges the Chinese position that there is but one China and Taiwan is part of China.

"Both believe that normalization of Sino-American relations is not only in the interest of the Chinese and American people but also contributes to the cause of peace in Asia and in the world.

"The United States of America and the People's Republic of China will exchange ambassadors and establish embassies on March 1, 1979."

Yesterday, our country and the People's Republic of China reached this final historic agreement. On Jan. 1, 1979, a little more than two weeks from now, our two governments will implement full normalization of diplomatic relations.

As a nation of gifted people who comprise about one-fourth of the total population of the Earth, China plays, already, an important role in world affairs—a role that can only grow more important in the years ahead.

We do not undertake this important step for transient tactical or expedient reasons. In recognizing the People's Republic of China—that it is a single government of China, we're recognizing simple reality. But far more is involved in this decision than just the recognition of a fact.

Before the estrangement of recent decades, the American and the Chinese people had a long history of friendship. We've already begun to rebuild some of the previous ties.

Now our rapidly expanding relationship requires a kind of structure that only full diplomatic relations will make possible.

The change that I'm announcing tonight will be of great long-term benefit to the peoples of both our country and China and I believe for all the peoples of the world.

Normalization and expanded commercial and cultural relations that it will bring will contribute to the well-being of our nation to our own national interest. And it will also enhance the stability of Asia.

These more positive relations with China can beneficially affect the world in which we live and the world in which our children will live.

We have already begun to inform our allies and other nations and the members of the Congress of the details of our intended action, but I wish also tonight to convey a special message to the people of Taiwan.

I have already communicated with the leaders in Taiwan, with whom the American people have had, and will have, extensive, close and friendly relations. This is important between our two peoples. As the United States asserted in the Shanghai Communiqué of 1972, issued on President Nixon's historic visit, we will continue to have an interest in the peaceful resolution of the Taiwan issue.

I have paid special attention to insuring that normalization of relations between our country and the People's Republic will not jeopardize the well-being of the people of Taiwan.

The people of our country will maintain our current commercial, cultural, trade and other relations with Taiwan through nongovernmental means. Many other countries of the world are already successfully doing this.

These decisions and these actions open a new and important chapter in our country's history and also in world affairs. To strengthen and to expedite the benefits of this new relationship between China and the United States, I am pleased to announce that Vice Premier Teng [Hsiao-ping] has accepted my invitation and will visit Washington at the end of January. His visit will give our governments the opportunity to consult with each other on global issues and to begin working together to enhance the cause of world peace.

These events are the final result of long and serious negotiations begun by President Nixon in 1972 and continued under the leadership of President Ford. The results bear witness to the steady, determined, bipartisan effort of our own country to build a world in which peace will be the goal and the responsibility of all nations.

The normalization of relations between the United States and China has no other purpose than the advancement of peace. It is in this spirit, at this season of peace, that I take special pride in sharing this good news with you tonight.

Thank you very much.

Taiwan Denounces the Accord

The U.S. decision to establish diplomatic relations with Peking provoked an angry denunciation from the Chinese Nationalists in Taiwan. President Chiang Ching-kuo Dec. 16, 1978 summoned U.S. Ambassador Leonard Unger to lodge a protest. Chiang later briefed his Cabinet ministers and then convened an emergency meeting of the Central Committee of the Kuomintang, the governing party.

A communique issued after the meeting said: "The decision by the United States to establish diplomatic relations with the Chinese Communist regime has not only seriously damaged the rights of the government and people of the Republic of China, but also has had tremendous adverse impact upon the free world."

In a statement of his own, President Chiang recalled that the U.S. had promised the Nationalists in the past few years that it would maintain relations with them and honor its treaty commitments. "Now that it has broken the assurances and abrogated the treaty, the United States government cannot be expected to have the confidence of any free nation in the future," he said. But Chiang moderated his tone somewhat in a television address later Dec. 16. He said: "I want to thank all those friends in America who have supported us. From now on the Republic of China will continue to strengthen the friendship and mutual interests of the two people."

The U.S. recognition of Peking prompted the Taiwan government to suspend indefintely Legislative Council and National Assembly elections scheduled for Dec. 23. And Foreign Minister Shen Chang-huan resigned in protest against the U.S. action, it was reported Dec. 16.

An anti-U.S. demonstration was staged Dec. 16 in front of the American embassy and U.S. military headquarters in Taipei. U.S. Marines guarding the embassy were reported to have driven back charging demonstrators with tear gas. Two guards were hurt during scuffles. As a result of the rioting, the U.S. embassy warned Americans Dec. 17 to stay off the streets of Taipei. About 1,000 persons demonstrated in front of the embassy Dec. 17, but no violence was reported.

President Chiang Dec. 18 again denounced the U.S., asserting that it had made "an unwise and horrible move" in agreeing to recognize China. The U.S., Chiang continued, had "never severed its relations with a friendly country. Now it has done that to the Republic of China. Shame on the United States." Speaking at the same meeting of the Kuomintang's Central Committee, Premier Sun Yun-suan pledged to increase the country's military spending "so that we can establish a self-sustaining defense industry."

President Chiang also had said that his government would not negotiate with Peking after it opened diplomatic relations with the U.S. Chiang's statement was in response to what appeared to be Peking's conciliatory gestures in the previous two days. An editorial in the Dec. 17 issue of the Communist Party newspaper *Jenmin Jih Pao* assured Taiwan that "the day will definitely come when Taiwan will return to the embrace of the motherland and our fellow countrymen will reunite with their kith and kin on the mainland." In contrast to previous Peking threats to "liberate" Taiwan, the party journal said there were "many patriots among the military and administrative personnel in Taiwan who will certainly make their own contribution to Taiwan's return to the motherland." Chairman Hua Kuo-feng had said Dec. 16 that "patriots belong to one family, whether they come early or late."

Statements on Washington-Peking Ties

Following are the texts of statements on U.S.-Chinese relations made by the U.S., Chinese Communist Party Chairman Hua Kuo-feng and Nationalist Chinese President Chiang Ching-kuo, made public Dec. 17, 1978:

United States Statement

As of Jan. 1, 1979, the United States of America recognizes the People's Republic of China as the sole legal government of China. On the same date, the People's Republic of China accords similar recognition to the United States of America. The United States of America thereby establishes diplomatic relations with the People's Republic of China.

On that same date, Jan. 1, 1979, the United States of America will notify Taiwan that it is terminating diplomatic relations and that the Mutual Defense Treaty between the United States and the Republic of China is being terminated in accordance with the provisions of the treaty. The United States also states that it will be withdrawing its remaining military personnel from Taiwan within four months.

In the future, the American people and the people of Taiwan will maintain commercial, cultural, and other relations without official government representation and without diplomatic relations.

The Administration will seek adjustments to our laws and regulations to permit the maintenance of commercial, cultural, and other nongovernmental relationships in the new circumstances that will exist after normalization.

The United States is confident that the people of Taiwan face a peaceful and prosperous future. The United States continues to have an interest in the peaceful resolution of the Taiwan issue and expects that the Taiwan issue will be settled peacefully by the Chinese themselves.

The United States believes that the establishment of diplomatic relations with the People's Republic will contribute to the welfare of the American people, to the stability of Asia where the United States has major security and economic interests and to the peace of the entire world.

Chinese Statement

As of Jan. 1, 1979, the People's Republic of China and the United States of America recognize each other and establish diplomatic relations, thereby ending the prolonged abnormal relationship between them. This is an historic event in Sino-United States relations.

As is known to all, the government of the People's Republic of China is the sole legal government of China and Taiwan is a part of China. The question of Taiwan was the crucial issue obstructing the normalizatin of relations between China and the United States. It has now been resolved between the two countries in the spirit of the Shanghai Communiqué and through their joint efforts, thus enabling the normalization of relations so ardently desired by the people of the two countries.

As for the way of bringing Taiwan back to the embrace of the motherland and reunifying the country, it is entirely China's internal affairs.

At the invitation of the U.S. Government, Teng Hsiao-ping, Deputy Prime Minister of the State Council of the People's Republic of China, will pay an official visit to the United States in January 1979, with a view to further promoting the friendship between the two peoples and good relations between the two countries.

Taiwan Statement

The decision by the United States to establish diplomatic relations with the Chinese Communist regime has not only seriously damaged the rights and interests of the government and the people of the Republic of China, but has also had a tremendously adverse impact upon the entire free world. For all the consequences that might arise as a result of this move, the United States government alone should bear full responsibility.

In the past few years, the United States government has repeatedly reaffirmed its intention to maintain diplomatic relations with the Republic of China and to honor its treaty commitments. Now that it has broken the assurances and abrogated the treaty, the United States government cannot be expected to have the confidence of any free nation in the future.

The United States, by extending diplomatic recognition to the Chinese Communist regime, which owes its very existence to terror and suppression, is not in conformity with its professed position of safeguarding human rights and strengthening the capability of democratic nations to resist the totalitarian dictatorship.

The move is tantamount to denying the hundreds of millions of enslaved peoples on the Chinese mainland of their hope for an early restoration of freedom. Viewed from whatever aspect, the move by the United States constitutes a great setback to human freedom and democratic institutions. It will be condemned by all freedom-loving and peace-loving peoples all over the world.

Recent international events have proven that the United States' pursuance of the "normalization" process with the Chinese Communist regime did not protect the security of free Asian nations, has further encouraged Communist subversion and aggressive activities and hastened the fall of Indochina into Communist hands. The government and the people of the Republic of China firmly believe lasting international peace and security can never be established on an unstable foundation of expediency.

Regardless of how the international situation may develop, the Republic of China, as a sovereign nation will, with her glorious tradition, unite all her people, civilian and military, at home and abroad, to continue her endeavors toward progress in the social, economic and political fields. The Chinese Government and the people, faithful to the national objectives and their international responsibilities, have full confidence in the future of the Republic of China.

The late President Chiang Kai-shek repeatedly instructed the Chinese people to be firm with dignity and to complete the task of national recovery and reconstruction. The Government and the people of the Republic of China have the determination and the faith, which they will exert their utmost, to work together with other free peoples in democratic countries to conquer Communist tyrannical rule and its aggressive policy. Henceforth, we shall be calm and firm, positive and hardworking. It is urged that all citizens cooperate fully with the government, with one heart and one soul, united and determined to fight at this difficult moment. Under whatever circumstances, the Republic of China shall neither negotiate with the Communist Chinese regime, nor compromise with Communism, and it shall never give up its sacred task of recovering the mainland and delivering the compatriots there. This firm position shall remain unchanged.

Mixed Reaction from U.S.

The sudden shift in the Carter Administration's China policy drew mixed reaction from domestic sources. The support for the President's action was muted in tone, although widespread. By contrast, there was vocal opposition, much of it strident and angry.

A "cowardly act," said Sen. Barry Goldwater (R, Ariz.) Dec. 15, 1978. "Disgraceful," "selfish and intemperate," said Republican National Chairman William Brock. "The plain fact" was, said Sen. Jesse A. Helms (R, N.C.) Dec. 15, that Carter "proposed to sell Taiwan down the river." The opposition was focused mainly on this issue—abandonment of the 23-year-old mutual defense treaty with Taiwan.

Goldwater, who jumped immediately into the lead of the opposition, said in his statement Dec. 15 that the President's decision "stabs in the back the nation of Taiwan, one of the most faithful and trustworthy friends our country has ever had." Goldwater warned that "if the President attempts to circumvent the Congress in abrogating our defense treaty with Taiwan, I plan to take him to court and show the action to be both illegal and unconstitutional." The Constitution stated that the president "shall have power, by and with the advice and consent of the Senate, to make treaties, provided two thirds of the senators present concur." But the Constitution was silent on termination of treaties. Goldwater's argument was that Carter's act was an abuse of presidential power, that he could not give notice of intent to terminate the treaty without approval by a two-thirds majority of the Senate or a simple majority of both houses.

Goldwater urged the Senate leadership Dec. 18 to seek a special session of Congress to deal with the issue. The termination of the treaty was scheduled to occur while Congress was in adjournment, he said, and a special session was necessary in view of "the disrespect shown Congress by the President in calling for action on a treaty that he has, in my opinion, no legal right to act upon unilaterally." Three Republican members of the House—John Ashbrook (Ohio), Robert Bauman (Md.) and Steven Symms (Idaho)—announced Dec. 20 that they were considering joining the Goldwater suit on the Taiwan defense treaty.

The lack, or inadequacy, of Administration consultation with Congress before acting also was a sticking point with members of Congress. Rep. Lester Wolff (D, N.Y.), who supported the establishment of diplomatic relations with the People's Republic of China and believed Carter had the legal right to break the Taiwan treaty, said Dec. 20, "I am unhappy with the methods used to inform Congress of the decision and the failure by the Administration to consult the Congress on the substance of the decision." Senate Republican leader Howard H. Baker Jr. (Tenn.) said Dec. 19 that "time must be given for Congress to deal with such an important foreign policy matter." Baker urged the President to delay giving notice of intention to end the Taiwan treaty. In a statement Dec. 16, Baker said, "The Taiwanese have been a good and faithful ally, and we certainly owe them more than this."

Zbigniew Brzezinski, Carter's national security adviser, defended the Administration's behavior in negotiating the matter more or less outside public notice. Appearing before the Foreign Policy Association Dec. 20, he said, "I think the American people are mature enough to realize that you cannot conduct negotiations and, at the same time, advertise every single step in the negotiating process. This would simply prevent negotiations."

AFL-CIO President George Meany, in a stern denunciation of Carter's action, brought up another issue of objection—human rights. What he could not understand, Meany said Dec. 20, was "how this President, who made human rights a world issue, could so suddenly and callously reject the human rights concerns of both those enslaved on mainland China and those on Taiwan who fear such enslavement."

President Carter admitted to reporters, after his televised address Dec. 15, that there had been a "mixed response" from congressional leaders when he had met with them earlier that evening. The support expressed publicly, however, was bipartisan. Sen. Edward M. Kennedy (D. Mass.) was one of those expressing approval Dec. 16. Another was House Republican Leader John J. Rhodes (Ariz.). Rep. John B. Anderson (R, Ill.) Dec. 16 called the establishment of U.S. diplomatic relations with the People's Republic of China an "historical inevitability."

Among those opposing the move were Sens. Bob Dole (R, Kan.) and Orrin Hatch (R, Utah), who appeared at a press conference Dec. 20 sponsored by the American Security Council. Sen. Jacob Javits (R, N.Y.), while not disapproving Dec. 15 of the action, called it "precipitate." It might "raise more questions than it settles regarding the security and stability of the area and the assurances given our allies, especially Japan and South Korea," Javits said. A Democratic member of the Senate Foreign Relations Committee, Sen. Richard Stone (Fla.), said Dec. 17 that "what the Senate and I can try to do is to repair the damage done to our credibility as an ally and to strengthen the situation on Taiwan."

Outside of Congress, former President Gerald R. Ford and former Secretary of State Henry A. Kissinger Dec. 15 expressed mild approval of Carter's decision. Kissinger also noted the "moral obligations" of the U.S. to the people of Taiwan. Ronald Reagan, contender against Ford for the 1976 Republican presidential nomination, protested Dec. 16 that "concrete reassurances" should be extended to the people of Taiwan.

The White House admitted Dec. 19 that public reaction to the President's decision was running four to one against it as measured by incoming mail and phone calls. According to a *New York Times* and CBS News poll released Dec. 19, however, respondents to a nationwide telephone survey were neither enthusiastic about closer ties with China nor about supporting Taiwan.

Wary Reaction from the Soviets

The reactions from European capitals to the new Washington—Peking ties were on the whole favorable. British Foreign Secretary David Owen Dec. 16, 1978 responded to Carter's announcement by saying that he was "delighted." The move, he said, was "overdue" and could help to create an "atmosphere of detente between the Soviet Union and China...." However, British Conservatives stressed the need for arming China as a buffer against the Soviet Union.

West Germany reacted favorably to the move Dec. 16, but there was no official comment from France. The French newspaper *Le Monde* that day said President Valery Giscard d'Estaing had been told in October of U.S. intentions by U.S. national security adviser Zbigniew Brzezinski.

The reactions of countries in Asia were generally positive also. Carter had telephoned Japanese Premier Masayoshi

Ohira one hour before announcing the U.S.-China normalization. Ohira had expressed optimism that the move would contribute to Asian stability. Thailand and the Philippines gave wholehearted approval Dec. 16. In addition, Thai Premier Kriangsak Chamanand said that he was satisfied that the U.S. "is still interested in the welfare of the people of Taiwan, with whom they intend to maintain . . . unofficial relations." A spokesman for the South Korean Foreign Ministry said Dec. 15 that the U.S.-China normalization was "not a surprising development." Seoul recently had permitted South Korean businessmen to seek trade with China, although efforts to establish commercial ties had not been successful.

On the other hand, the Soviet Union looked on the development with skeptical eyes. Anatoly Dobrynin, Soviet ambassador to the U.S., was briefed on the U.S.-China developments Dec. 15 by Brzezinski. According to reports of the meeting, Brzezinski had assured Dobrynin that the U.S.-China ties were not directed against the U.S.S.R. *Pravda*, the Soviet Communist Party newspaper, expressed doubt over Brzezinski's pledge. "Time will show whether these words accord with practical deeds and political action," the newspaper said. *Pravda* concluded that the U.S. move was "a result of changes in the orientation of the Peking leadership," especially its "open antagonism toward the world of socialism and an alliance with the most bellicose circles of the West." *Pravda* warned the West against seeking to reinforce Peking militarily against the Soviet Union. It said China was "in no hurry to accept the American interpretation" that U.S.-China relations did not threaten any third country.

Earlier, Soviet analysts had expressed concern that U.S.-Chinese ties might be used against the Soviet Union. Georgi Arbatov, the leading Soviet expert on the U.S., was quoted as saying in November that U.S.-Chinese relations were "a very serious test for the political wisdom and intention of the West." In an interview with the *International Herald Tribune* (Paris) Arbatov warned the West against the "temptation" to use China against the Soviet Union. "If China becomes some sort of military ally to the West, even an informal ally . . . on an anti-Soviet basis, then there is no place for detente, even in a narrow sense."

Nevertheless, the Soviets' official reaction as communicated to the White House was polite. President Carter said Dec. 19 that he had received a "very positive" reaction from Soviet President Leonid Brezhnev to the U.S. decision to establish diplomatic relations with the People's Republic of China. Speaking in a CBS-TV interview, the President said Brezhnev had conveyed his reaction in a "personal message" delivered to the White House that day. Carter and Brezhnev had agreed that the U.S.'s "new relationship with the People's Republic of China will contribute to world peace" and "the proper relationship between major sovereign nations is to have full diplomatic relations." The President assured listeners that "our new relationship with China will not put any additional obstacles in the way of a successful SALT [strategic arms limitation talks] agreement and also will not endanger our good relationship with the Soviet Union."

The Soviet Union indicated Dec. 21 that Brezhnev's personal note to Carter Dec. 19 on U.S.-Chinese relations was not as positive as Carter led the public to believe. In disclosing details of Brezhnev's message, the Soviet news agency Tass said that the Soviet leader had expressed concern about a passage in the joint U.S.-Chinese communique opposing "hegemony," a Chinese term for Soviet expansionism. Tass said that Brezhnev had "taken notice" of Carter's promise not to use the new U.S.-Chinese relationship against Soviet interests and stressed that normal diplomatic ties between sovereign nations was a "natural matter." However, it was "another question," Tass added, "on what basis the normalization takes place.... This question is also natural, especially bearing in mind the quite definite trend of China's present course." In view of this, the news agency reported, Brezhnev's note "draws attention to the fact that the joint American-Chinese communique contains expressions whose direction is beyond doubt, if one bears in mind the usual vocabulary of the Chinese leaders," a clear allusion by Tass to the term "hegemony." Brezhnev had told Carter that Moscow would "closely follow" the direction of U.S.-Chinese relations and "from this will draw appropriate conclusions for Soviet policy," Tass said.

Commenting on the Soviet statement, Presidential Press Secretary Jody Powell said Dec. 21 that the White House, like

Tass, would not release the text of Brezhnev's message to Carter. Asked by newsmen why Carter had not indicated any reservations by Brezhnev about U.S.-Chinese relations, Powell replied that he did not think the President "sought to give you a paragraph-by-paragraph rundown."

Subsequently, U.S. national security adviser Brzezinski and Secretary of State Vance offered different interpretations of the effect of the new U.S. ties with Peking on U.S. relations with the Soviet Union. They made their remarks at a State Department meeting Jan. 15, 1979 with businessmen.

Vance assured his audience that the U.S. will "insure continuity of trade, cultural and other unofficial relations" with Taiwan. He said Washington-Peking relations would promote "a stable system of independent nations in Asia" and "a stable equilibrium among the United States, Japan, China and the Soviet Union." Vance declared that the U.S. "acted in a way that does not threaten any other nation," referring to the U.S.S.R. He said both China and the Soviet Union have "an important role to play in the search for global peace and stability." "For this reason," Vance concluded, "we also look forward to the early conclusion of the SALT agreement with the Soviet Union and to improvement of our trade relations with the Soviets as well as the Chinese."

Brzezinski, who followed Vance, echoed the secretary of state's emphasis on multilateral cooperation with China and the Soviet Union. However, he stressed the strategic significance of the U.S.-Chinese ties. Expressing his doubts about the Soviet's policy, Brzezinski said that "a fundamental choice the Soviet Union faces is whether to become a responsible partner in the creation of a global system of genuinely independent states or whether to exclude itself from global trends and derive its security exclusively from its military might and its domination of a few clients." He declared that "whichever path the Soviet Union chooses, we will continue our efforts to shape a framework for global cooperation based not on domination but on respect for diversity."

Recognition & Peace Feelers

As announced, the U.S. and the People's Republic of China formally established diplomatic relations Jan. 1, 1979. At the same time, the U.S. severed its ties with the Chinese Nationalist government on Taiwan.

The resumption of formal diplomatic relations was celebrated in simultaneous receptions at the U.S. and Chinese liaison offices in Peking and Washington. The ceremony in the Chinese capital was attended by a large Chinese delegation headed by Deputy Premier Teng Hsiao-ping and by Leonard Woodcock, head of the U.S. liaison office, who had negotiated the final agreement on normalization.

Teng said in a toast in Peking that it was "a particularly memorable day for the Chinese and American peoples. It marks the end of the prolonged abnormal state in Sino-U.S. relations." In his toast, Woodcock said, "We believe that today marks a new era in our relations that will contribute to the well-being of both countries and all mankind."

At the Washington reception, U.S. Vice President Walter F. Mondale said China and the U.S. were brought together by "an awareness of our parallel interests in creating a world of economic progress, stability and peace." The head of the Chinese liaison office, Chai Tse-min, called the establishment of diplomatic relations "an event of historic significance." He added that "it is our firm conviction that as time goes by the friendship of the Chinese and American peoples and the good relations of the two countries will certainly continue to be consolidated and strengthened."

Peking marked the occasion by extending anew a hand of reconciliation to Taiwan. It offered Dec. 31, 1978 to establish trade and other links with Taiwan. This offer was met with immediate rejection in Taipei. A Nationalist government spokesman said Jan. 1 that "under no circumstances will we enter into any kind of talks with the Chinese Communists."

In another peace overture to Taiwan, Peking Jan 4. offered to permit Nationalist Chinese airliners to land at Peking and Shanghai. A Taiwan official rejected the offer, saying that "it is this government's policy not to negotiate, compromise, trade or whatever with Communist China—not to mention flying our planes to the mainland."

President Chiang Ching-kuo of Nationalist China Jan. 1 called for his country's reconquest of the Chinese mainland. "The responsibility of carrying out the historic task of recovering the mainland and delivering from Communist slavery and tyranny compatriots whose blood is the same as ours rests squarely on the shoulders of each of our 17 million people." Chiang said.

Deputy Premier Teng Hsiao-ping conferred in Peking Jan. 2 with a visiting delegation of eight U.S. congressmen, all members of the House Banking Committee. One of the representatives, Thomas L. Ashley (D, Ohio), quoted Teng as having said that "the reunification of China and Taiwan would be peaceful and the standard of living of the people of Taiwan would be maintained." Ashley said Teng had made it clear that "China does not plan to pursue a strong-armed policy, although he said that [reunification] remained an internal matter of China."

Teng also invited Sen. Barry Goldwater (R, Ariz.), a leading opponent of the U.S. decision to recognize the People's Republic of China, to visit Peking. According to Ashley, Teng said "he would make a point of engaging in a . . . conversation with the senator on this or any other matter."

In another conversation Teng had Jan. 9 with a group of visiting U.S. senators—Sam Nunn (D, Ga.), Gary W. Hart (D, Colo.), William Cohen (R, Me.) and John Glenn (D, Ohio)— the deputy premier offered to allow Taiwan to retain its own government and armed forces in exchange for ceding sovereignty after it was unified with the Chinese mainland.

A statement issued by the American delegation on its conversation with Teng said: "It was indicated that Taiwan would retain full autonomy with China for as long as the people of Taiwan would so desire, and in the future Taiwan authorities would possess the same powers they now enjoy." As for the Chinese Nationalists' armed forces, "there would be no requirement that Taiwan disarm in order to achieve reunification," the statement continued. The senators also said that Teng had "indicated that China would not use force to change the system and way of life on Taiwan," except under two circumstances: in the event of "an indefinite refusal by Taiwan to enter into negotiations" with Peking on its future relations with China, and, in case of "an attempt by the Soviet Union to interfere in Taiwanese affairs."

This new overture, as previous ones, was immediately spurned by the Nationalist government in Taipei. The Nationalist Premier Sun Yen-suan Jan. 11 rejected Teng's proposals on reunificaton, asserting that his suggestion for negotiations was "merely another form of class struggle."

Teng Visits U.S.

If these repeated peace overtures from Peking failed to move the Nationalists on Taiwan, they nevertheless helped to alleviate the concern in the U.S. about the security of Taiwan, thus smoothing the way for Chinese Deputy Premier Teng Hsiao-ping's visit to the U.S.

Teng arrived in Washington Jan. 28, 1979 to start the first official call to the U.S. by a top Chinese Communist leader. Teng held a series of talks with President Carter at the White House Jan. 29-30, and the two men Jan. 31 signed agreements on cultural and scientific exchanges. The accords included:

■ Agreement on the establishment of U.S. consulates in Shanghai and Canton and Chinese consulates in Houston and San Francisco and provisions for reuniting families and protecting citizens if arrested. (This agreement was signed by Secretary of State Cyrus Vance and Foreign Minister Huang Hua.)

■ An overall science and technology pact, and a separate energy agreement providing for U.S. assistance in constructing a nuclear-particle accelerator in China.

■ A space technology accord enabling China to purchase services of the U.S.' National Aeronautics & Space Administration for launching a civilian communications satellite.

■ A cultural agreement aimed at increasing contacts and exchanges in a wide variety of fields.

■ A science agreement providing for the exchange of students.

In addition to these formal accords, Peking also agreed in principle to permit American news organizations to set up bureaus in China.

Carter called the agreements "a new and irreversible course" in Chinese-American relations. While both nations "have agreed to consult regularly on matters of common global interest," Carter conceded that "the security concerns of the United States do not coincide completely, of course, with those of China, nor does China share our responsibilities." Teng praised the agreements as "significant." He asserted, however, that "this is not the end but just a beginning." He added, "there are many more areas of bilateral cooperation and more channels waiting for us to develop."

Teng Jan. 29 had stressed what he called the Soviet menace to world peace. He did so in a speech at a full-dress welcoming ceremony on the White House lawn before his first session with Carter. Without mentioning the Soviets by name, Teng warned Carter that the threat of war was increasing and that "our two countries are duty bound to work together" to maintain peace. (Before leaving for the U.S., Teng had depicted the Soviet Union in a *Time* magazine [Feb. 5 issue] interview as "a hotbed of war" and warned that Moscow's military strength "may surpass that of the United States in the near future." As a result, he advised the U.S. not to sign any agreement limiting weapons development.)

After the Jan 29 session, the White House announced that Carter had accepted an invitation from Teng to visit China and that Teng had accepted an invitation from the President for Communist Party Chairman Hua Kuo-feng to visit the U.S. No dates were set for either trip.

The U.S. and China Feb. 1 issued a joint press communique on the Carter-Teng talks, which indirectly criticized the Soviet Union. The criticism, however, was softened at Washington's insistence. The Chinese had demanded the incorporation into the text of the word "hegemony," Peking's term for Soviet expansionism. The U.S. had insisted on adding the word "domination," which would appear to cover aggression in general. As a result, the communique read that the U.S. and China "reaffirm they are opposed to efforts by any country or group of countries to establish hegemony or domination over others." The document also took note of the accords signed by Carter and Teng. The press communique was issued at the request of the Chinese, who argued that it would be less formal or binding than an official joint statement.

Secretary of State Cyrus Vance conferred later Feb. 1 with Soviet Ambassador Anatoly F. Dobrynin to assure him that the Carter-Teng talks and the communique were not aimed at forging a Washington-Peking alignment against Moscow.

Meeting with 85 U.S. senators on Capitol Hill Jan. 30, Teng spoke of possible Chinese military action against Taiwan and Vietnam. China, he said, hoped to unite Taiwan with the mainland by peaceful means and would "fully respect the realities" of the island. But the deputy premier said he could not categorically rule out the use of force to regain Taiwan because it would restrict his government's options in proposed reunification talks with the Chinese Nationalists. Teng also left open the possibility of China's use of force against Vietnam to settle a dispute stemming from Vietnam's invasion of Cambodia and Chinese-Vietnamese border tensions. One senator quoted him as having said that to safeguard China's borders, "we need to act appropriately, we cannot allow Vietnam to run wild everywhere." Vietnam, Teng said, was seeking "regional hegemony," a term meaning expansionism to the Chinese.

A senator who opposed the U.S.' severing of its ties with Taiwan, Jesse Helms (R, N.C.), said Teng had "evaded" his question as to whether China would avoid employing military action, an economic boycott, "or other forms of coercion" against Taiwan. "What he is saying is, of course, somewhere down the line we are going to use force," Helms said.

Teng reiterated his warning against Vietnam at a luncheon with reporters Jan. 31. China, he said, was prepared to use military force against Vietnam because of its invasion of Cambodia and its violations of the Chinese border. "If you don't teach them some necessary lessons, it just won't do," he said.

Outside the official world of presidential meetings and communiques, Teng's visit to Washington was considered by most observers to have been a diplomatic tour de force. Moving affably through a series of meetings, luncheons and private discussions, Teng displayed a charm, wit and candor that gained immediate rapport with his American audiences. One of the few dissenters was Sen. Helms, who had attended the Senate luncheon with Teng Jan. 30. "He didn't help himself a bit with me," Helm asserted. A more general reaction was that

Teng was "an impressive man.... He's making a favorable impression today," as Sen. John Tower (R, Tex.) observed. (Yet Tower, like Helms, was staunchly on Taiwan's side in its antagonism to the mainland Chinese government.) Rep. Jack Brooks (D, Tex.) agreed, following Teng's appearance at a reception with House members Jan. 30. "He made a pretty good statement for helping his position up here," Brooks said. Teng also met privately Jan. 30 with Democratic leaders of both houses of Congress.

The only jarring event during Teng's Washington visit took place during the full-dress welcoming ceremony Jan. 29 at the White House, an event attended by several thousand people. The ceremony was disrupted briefly by a young woman and a young man, who suddenly began shouting denunciations of Teng from the press gallery platform only 35 feet from Carter and Teng. Dragged away immediately by uniformed White House policemen, they were identified later as members of the Revolutionary Communist Party (RCP), a Maoist group. Both had official press credentials to gain admission to the ceremony.

That evening 40 other members of the RCP were arrested outside the White House during the only violent demonstration of a day of anti-Teng demonstrations by various groups, most of them pro-Taiwan or communist. Other demonstrators Jan. 29 included several dozen protesting the return of former President Richard M. Nixon to the White House that evening. Nixon was a guest at a state dinner for Teng at the White House. Nixon's secretary of state, Henry A. Kissinger, was another guest at the dinner. The Chinese officials, including Teng, had asked for an opportunity to meet with Nixon because of his role in opening up Chinese-U.S. relations.

Teng was especially effective with his down-to-earth manner during lunch with 11 reporters Jan. 31, when he offered thumbnail sketches of himself and President Carter. "You can say I'm from the country, not a city slicker," he said. As for Carter, he found him "easy to get along with." Teng even gave the reporters something of a scoop by disclosing that he had two grandchildren, a four-year-old boy and a girl, almost six. Up to then, U.S. experts on China had known of only one grandchild. "At home they give orders, and I have to obey their orders," said Teng.

Teng had been greeted on his arrival at the airport Jan. 28 by Vice President Walter F. Mondale, Secretary of State Vance and several members of Congress. That evening, Teng and his wife, Cho Lin, were dinner guests of Zbigniew Brzezinski, the President's national security adviser. The evening was described as "an informal reunion of the negotiating team" that had worked out the normalization of relations between the two countries. Leonard Woodcock, head of the U.S. mission in Peking, was one of the guests.

A gala was staged for Teng at Kennedy Center Jan. 29. The performers included the Harlem Globetrotters basketball team, who put on their famous ball-handling routine to the tune of *Sweet Georgia Brown.* Teng's busy day Jan. 31 included a morning visit by Nixon to Blair House, where Teng was staying, visits by Teng to the National Air & Space Museum and the Lincoln Memorial and a visit that evening from Prince Norodom Sihanouk of Cambodia.

Teng ended his nine-day trip to the U.S. with visits to Atlanta, Houston and Seattle Feb. 1-5. Teng's tour of the three industrial American centers dramatized China's quest for U.S. technological aid in its drive toward modernization.

During his one-day stay in Atlanta Feb. 1 the deputy premier addressed a group of notables, toured a Ford Motor Co. assembly plant, met with Southern newspaper publishers and editors and laid a wreath at the grave of civil rights leader Dr. Martin Luther King Jr. In a luncheon speech before a gathering of 1,400 business and civil leaders, Teng said, "There is much in your experience from which we can benefit. We would like to learn from you." But he returned to his constant theme of Soviet foreign policy, asserting that "hegemonism is the greatest threat to international peace and stability." Among those attending the luncheon were King's widow, Coretta Scott King, former Secretary of State Dean Rusk and Georgia Governor George Busbee. At the Ford Motor Co. plant, Teng was escorted by Leonard Woodcock, head of the U.S. liaison office in Peking, and he was greeted by company Chairman Henry Ford II, who had come from Detroit for the occasion.

On arriving in Houston Feb. 2, Teng emphasized the commercial advantages he hoped to find in the city. He described it as a "center of the petroleum industry" and expressed his eagerness to "learn about your advanced experience in the petroleum industry and other fields." Teng was accompanied to Houston by Secretary of Energy James Schlesinger. Teng was taken on a three-hour tour of the Lyndon B. Johnson Space Center, where he took the controls of a space ship on a simulated mission. He also rode in a model lunar rover and looked at an exhibit of moon rocks. Teng concluded his day by attending a barbecue and a rodeo in nearby Simonton, Texas.

Teng ended his visit to Houston Feb. 3 with a tour of the Hughes Tool Co., manufacturer of oil drills. At a meeting with newspaper editors and publishers, the Chinese leader reported progress in negotiations with the U.S. to help develop China's oil resources. At least six American companies were involved in the talks. Teng said China would need billions of dollars in foreign exchange for its modernization plans. The U.S. position on the China-Taiwan question appeared to underline Teng's presence in Houston. Conservative Texas political leaders were said to be concerned that their appearance with Teng might be construed as endorsement of the Carter Administration's decision to end diplomatic relations with Taiwan. Texas Sen. Lloyd Bentsen (D) had originally been scheduled to accompany Teng on the flight from Atlanta to Houston, but then said he had a previous commitment in Texas. Bentsen, as well as his fellow Texan senator, John Tower (R), were absent from a rodeo staged for Teng Feb. 2.

Teng flew Feb. 4 to Seattle, where he spent the last full day in the U.S. concentrating on the aviation industry. He inspected the Boeing Co. plant near the city, which was building three 747 jetliners for China. At a business luncheon sponsored by Boeing Co. and United Airlines, Teng again praised the industrial might of the U.S. China, he said, wanted "to learn from the American people, creators of an advanced civilization." He said the improvement of U.S.-Chinese relations "will certainly exert a positive and far-reaching influence on the situation in the Pacific region and in the world as a whole."

In an airport statement before leaving for home Feb. 5, Teng said he was going back "laden with warm sentiments of the

American people." He expressed hope that the Chinese and American people would "live in friendship from generation to generation" and would "always safeguard world peace together."

Statements Made During Teng's Visit

President Carter said in his welcoming remarks to Teng Jan. 29:

... Today we take another step in the historic normalization of relations which we have begun this year. We share in the hope which springs from reconciliation and the anticipation of a common journey. The United States of America has major interests in the Asian and in the Pacific regions. We expect that normalization of relations between our two countries will help to produce an atmosphere in the Asian and Pacific area in which the right of all peoples to live in peace will be enhanced. We expect that normalization will help to move us together toward a world of diversity and of peace. For too long, our two peoples were cut off from one another. Now we share the prospect of a fresh flow of commerce, ideas, and people, which will benefit both our countries.

Under the leadership of Premier Hua Kuo-feng and of you, Mr. Vice Premier, the People's Republic of China has begun to move boldly toward modernization. You have chosen to broaden your cultural, trade, and diplomatic ties with other nations. We welcome this openness. As a people, we firmly believe in open discussion with others and a free exchange of ideas with others. Our nation is made up of people of many backgrounds, brought together by a common belief in justice, individual liberty, and a willingness to settle differences peaceably. So, we particularly welcome the opportunity to exchange students and scholars and to improve our trade, technological, scientific, and cultural contacts. We are eager for you and your people to see and to experience our nation and for our people to experience yours. There is a Chinese saying that seeing once is worth more than a hundred descriptions. For too long, the Chinese and American peoples have not been able to see each other for themselves. We are glad that time is past.

China is one of the nations to which a significant number of Americans, our own citizens, trace their ancestry. The American people have warm feelings for the Chinese. But history also teaches us that our peoples have not always dealt with each other wisely. For the past century and more, our relations have often been marred by misunderstanding, false hopes, and even war. Mr. Vice Premier, let us pledge together that both the United States and China will exhibit the understanding, patience, and persistence which will be needed in order for our new relationship to survive. Our histories and our political and economic systems are vastly different. Let us recognize those differences and make them sources not of fear, but of healthy curiosity; not as a source of divisiveness, but of mutual benefit. As long as we harbor no illusions about our differences, our diversity can contibute to the validity of our new relationship. People who are different have much to learn from each other.

Yesterday, Mr. Vice Premier, was the lunar New Year, the beginning of your Spring Festival, the traditional time of new beginnings for the Chinese people. On your New Year's Day, I am told, you open all doors and windows to give access to beneficient spirits. It's a time when family quarrels are forgotten, a time when visits are made, a time of reunion and reconciliation. As for our two nations, today is a time of reunion and new beginnings. It's a day of reconciliation, when windows too long closed have been reopened. . . .

Replying to Carter's welcoming remarks, Teng said:

. . . This history of friendly contacts between our two peoples goes back for nearly 200 years, and what is more, we fought shoulder to shoulder in the war against fascism. Though there was a period of unpleasantness between us for 30 years, normal relations between China and the United States have at last been restored. . . . Great possibilities lie ahead for developing amicable cooperation between China and the United States. In the next few days, we will be exploring with your Government leaders and with friends in all walks of life ways to develop our contacts and cooperation in the political economic, scientific, technological, and cultural fields.

Normalization opens up broad vistas for developing these contacts and cooperation to our mutual benefit. We have every reason to expect fruitful results. The significance of normalization extends far beyond our bilateral relations. Amicable cooperation between two major countries, situated on opposite shores of the Pacific, is undoubtedly an important factor working for peace in this area and in the world as a whole. The world today is far from tranquil. There are not only threats to peace, but the factors making for war are visibly growing. The people of the world have the urgent task of redoubling their efforts to maintain world peace, security, and stability. And our two countries are duty-bound to work to gether and make our due contribution to that end.

Mr. President, we share the sense of being on an historic mission. Sino-U.S. relations have reached a new beginning, and the world situation is at a new turning point. China and the United States are great countries, and the Chinese and American peoples, two great peoples. Friendly cooperation between our two peoples is bound to exert a positive and far-reaching influence on the way the world situation evolves. . . . "

At a state dinner the evening of Jan. 29, Carter said:

. . . In the past year, more than 120 delegations from the People's Republic of China have come here to the United States to visit us. And an even greater number of American groups have left here and gone to visit China. Exchanges have already begun in the natural sciences, in space, in agriculture, in medicine, in science, in technology, and other fields. And now with the establishment of normal diplomatic relations, the exploratory nature of these many exchanges can give way to a more valuable and a more permanent relationship. This will serve the interests of both our nations and will also serve the cause of peace.

Today, for the first time since the establishment of normal diplomatic relations, the Governments of the United States of America and the People's Republic of China have begun official discussions at the highest level. ... We've not entered this new relationship for any short-term gains. We have a long-term commitment to a world community of diverse nations and independent nations. We believe that a strong and a secure China will play a cooperative part in developing that type of world community which we envision. Our new relationship particularly can contribute to the peace and stability of the Asia-Pacific region. ...

I know the shocks of change in my own life, and I know the sometimes painful adjustments required when change occurs, as well as the great potential for good that change can bring to both individuals and to nations. I know, too, that neither individuals nor nations can stifle change. It is far better to adapt scientific and technological advantages to our needs, to learn to control them, and to reap their benefits while minimizing their potential adverse effects. And I know that the Chinese people and you, Mr. Vice Premier, understand these things about change very well. Your ambitious modernization effort in four different areas of human life attests to that. The American people wish you well in these efforts, and we are looking forward to cooperating with you and with the people of China.

In his final message, the day before he died, Franklin Roosevelt—who would have been 97 years old tomorrow—wrote these words: "If civilization is to survive, we must cultivate the science of human relationships—the ability of people of all kinds to live together and to work together, in the same world and at peace." In that spirit, Mr. Vice Premier, I would like to propose a toast: To the newly established diplomatic relationships between the United States of America and the people of the republic of China; to the health of Premier Hua Kuo-feng; to the health of Vice Premier Teng and Madame Cho Lin; and to the further development of friendship between the people of China and the people of the United States of America.

Teng said in his reply:

... Our two countries have different social systems and ideologies, but both governments are aware that the interests of our peoples and of world peace require that we view our bilateral relations in the context of the overall international situation and with a long-term strategic perspective. This was the reason why the two sides easily reached agreement on normalization.

Moreover, in the Joint Communique on the Establishment of Diplomatic Relations, our two sides solemnly committed themselves that neither should seek hegemony and each was opposed to efforts by any other country or group of countries to establish such hegemony. This commitment restrains ourselves and adds to our sense of responsibility for world peace and stability. We are confident that the amicable cooperation between the Chnese and

American peoples is not only in the interest of our two countries' development but will also become a strong factor working for the preservation of
world peace and the promotion of human progress....

In his remarks following the signing of the U.S.-Chinese agreements Jan. 31, Carter said:

What we have accomplished in the last three days is truly exceptional. But
our aim is to make this kind of exchange between our countries no longer the
exception, but the norm; no longer a matter of headlines and historians, but a
routine part of the everyday lives of both the Chinese and the American
people. With the signing of these agreements, we have begun to do just
exactly that....

... While we pursue independent foreign policies, our separate actions in
many places can contribute to similar goals. These goals are a world of
security and peace, a world of both diversity and stability, a world of
independent nations free of outside domination. Both our countries have a
special interest in promoting the peace and prosperity of the people of East
Asia. We have agreed to consult regularly on matters of common global
interest. The security concerns of the United States do not coincide completely, of course, with those of China, nor does China share our responsibilities. But a strong and secure China which contributes constructively to world
affairs is in our interest, and a globally engaged, confident, and strong
America is, obviously, in China's interest.

The agreements that we have just signed for cultural, scientific and technological exchanges, and for consular arrangements will bring the tangible
benefits of normalization to increasing numbers of both our peoples. We
look forward to an early settlement of the issue of claims and assets, to the
reunification of families, to expanded tourism, and to the development of a
healthy and a vigorous trading relationship between our countries. In the
near future, because of these agreements, American consulates will open in
Shanghai and Canton, and Chinese consulates will open in Houston and San
Francisco. Hundreds of American students will study and will learn in China,
and hundreds of Chinese students will further their education in the United
States. Our National Aeronautics & Space Administration (NASA) will
launch a civilian communications satellite, paid for by China, that will bring
color television and expanded communications to all of the people of China
for the first time....

Teng said in his reply:

...We have just done a significant job. But this is not the end, but a
beginning. We anticipated that following the normalization of relations,
there would be a rapid development of friendly cooperation between our two
countries in many broad fields. The agreements we have just signed are the
first fruits of our endeavors. There are many more areas of bilateral coopera-

tion and many more channels waiting for us to develop. We have to continue our efforts.

It is my belief that extensive contacts and cooperation among nations and increased interchanges and understanding between peoples will make the world we live in more safe, more stable, and more peaceful. Therefore, the work we have just done is not only in the interests of the Chinese and American peoples but of the peoples of the world as well. It is with these remarks that I mark the signing of the agreement between China and the United States on scientific and technlogical cooperation, the cultural agreements, and other documents....

Consumation of New Relationship

Administrative measures to implement the U.S.-Chinese political decision followed Teng's visit.

The U.S. Senate voted Feb. 26, 1979 to confirm President Carter's nomination of Leonard Woodcock as U.S. ambassador to mainland China. The vote was 82 to 9. Woodcock was installed March 1 in Peking, becoming the first full-fledged American envoy there since 1949. He had headed the U.S. liaison mission, a provisional diplomatic office, for the previous two years. Several Republican senators, led by Sens. Jesse Helms (N.C.) and S. I. Hayakawa (Calif.), tried to use the Woodcock nomination as a way of protesting President Carter's China policies and the Chinese invasion of Vietnam. After it became apparent that the critics lacked the votes to block the nomination, they allowed the nomination to be voted on.

U.S. Secretary of the Treasury W. Michael Blumenthal arrived in Peking Feb. 24 to establish closer U.S.-Chinese economic relations. One of the issues to be settled concerned U.S. claims to the property seized by Communist China in 1949, estimated at $196.6 million. Blumenthal met with Chinese officials to conclude the negotiations prior to the formal opening of the U.S. embassy in Peking and of the Chinese embassy in Washington. An agreement was signed in Peking March 1 providing for China to pay the U.S. about 41¢ on the dollar.

The resolution of the assets issue was seen as an essential step in the establishment of normal economic ties between the two countries. Blumenthal described the accord as "good and fair." U.S. officials argued that the settlement was desirable because it would prevent the issue from being the subject of protracted litigation. The accord called for China to pay U.S. claimants a total of about $80.5 million: the first $30 million on Oct. 1 and the remainder in five yearly installments of $10 million each. In paying the claims, China would use the $80 million it had in assets that had been frozen by the U.S. If, as was likely, China was not able to recover all of those claims, it would have to use additional cash to settle the U.S. claims, the *Wall Street Journal* reported March 2. The agreement on assets required approval by Congress.

In addition to the agreement, China and the U.S. set up a joint economic committee to monitor commercial and financial relations between the two countries. The U.S. also invited the Bank of China to open an office in the U.S., a proposal to which the Chinese responded positively. The two nations agreed to "proceed rapidly," Blumenthal said, on negotiations to reach a bilateral trade agreement. They agreed that the accord should include reciprocal tariff concessions, provision for physical facilities for businessmen in China, patent and copyright protections and rules for deciding trade disputes.

The U.S. liaison office in Peking was officially upgraded to embassy status at noon March 1, with Blumenthal taking part in the ceremony. "The purpose for which I came to Peking as it relates to our economic relations has been achieved," Blumenthal said at the ceremony. The Chinese the same day officially opened their embassy in Washington. Ambassador Chai Tse-min, who had headed the Chinese liaison office in Washington, formally presented his credentials to President Carter in the Oval Office of the White House.

The U.S. also officially closed its embassy in Taipei, Taiwan March 1. The American Institute in Taiwan, which was to take over responsibility for the chores previously handled by the embassy, was unable to open because the U.S. Congress had not appropriated funds for its operations. It was not until well toward the end of March that Congress passed a bill that provided for unofficial relations between U.S. and Taiwan. The bill also contained some security assurance to the island. The House passed the measure March 28 by 339-50 vote, and the Senate approved it by 85-4 vote. The final compromise version of the bill tied the U.S. somewhat closer to Taiwan than the Carter Administration had intended. President Carter signed the legislation April 10.

The measure stated that the U.S. agreed to conduct its relations with Taiwan through a private corporation, the American Institute in Taiwan. The Nationalist Chinese continued their relations with the U.S. through an unofficial Coordinating Council in North America. The U.S.-Taiwan relations bill stated that all trade, cultural and transportation links between the two countries would continue. The bill said that the U.S. would take unspecified actions in the event of an attack on Taiwan, stronger language than President Carter had wanted. The bill further pledged continued arms sales to the Nationalists.

The government of the People's Republic of China had lodged an official protest against the Taiwan security provision of the bill March 16. It continued to voice its unhappiness over the provision after the bill was signed into law by President Carter. In a meeting with a group of visiting U.S. senators, Teng said April 19 that the measure came close to nullifying the normalization of relations between China and the U.S. Sen. Frank Church (D., Idaho), who led the delegation, said in an interview later that Teng was "very strong in saying this [legislation] is a violation" of the agreement reached in December 1978.

China Invades Vietnam

The Moscow-Hanoi Axis

The Taiwan issue receded into the background in the winter of 1978 as the Indochinese situation took a sharp turn for the worse. The Peking-Hanoi negotiations to settle the status of the ethnic Chinese in Vietnam had deteriorated into a snarling match. The Chinese massed troops within striking distance of Vietnam's northern provinces. In Cambodia, the Pol Pot government established at Pnompenh had its hands full with a domestic insurgency backed by Hanoi. In addition, its troops were engaged in armed clashes with better-equipped and better-trained Vietnamese forces along the Cambodian-Vietnamese borders. Not a day passed without Pnompenh radio reporting on Vietnamese incursion into Cambodian territory.

Pnompenh radio Oct. 18, 1978 told of new fighting between invading Vietnamese forces and Cambodian soldiers in the Parrot's Beak area of Cambodia near the Vietnamese border. The intruders were attacked and destroyed, the broadcast said. Cambodian Deputy Premier Ieng Sary accused the Soviet Union Oct. 19 of taking a direct role in Vietnamese attacks on his country as part of a "grand design" to dominate Southeast Asia. Ieng made the remark in Manila during a tour of Southeast Asia to seek moral support for his government. "This regional ambition agrees with the global ambition of the expansionist big power [the Soviet Union] who wanted to dominate all Southeast Asia, and in the framework of its world strategy, this expansionist big power ordered Vietnam to serve this ambition," Ieng said. He asserted that the Soviet Union had provided Vietnam with aid and advisers to attack Cambodia and that at the end of 1977 the bodies of two Soviet advisers had been found on a battlefield in Cambodia.

Meanwhile, Vietnamese-assisted Cambodian rebels staged uprisings against the Pol Pot regime at Pnompenh. Hanoi radio reported Oct. 23 that a rebellion had broken out in 16 of Cambodia's 19 provinces. According to the broadcast, rebel soldiers occupied all roads in the northeastern provinces of Ratanakiri and Stung Treng, severing supplies to Pnompenh. Other soldiers were said to have mutinied at the airport at

Kompong Cham, capital of the eastern border province of the same name. Fighting also occurred in the western military region where "insurrection forces attacked the towns of Kratie and Kompong Thom," the broadcast said. Hanoi radio claimed that people on state farms and in factories were holding meetings and demonstrations and distributing leaflets calling on the populace to rise up.

Tension was increasing in the north, along the Sino-Vietnamese borders, as well. Hanoi radio charged that Chinese troops Oct. 13 had killed two Vietnamese border guards and abducted another to China. The incident was said to have occurred in Vietnam's Hoang Lien Son province. Hanoi further accused Peking Oct. 18 of massing troops and building fortifications along their frontier in an attempt to give support to Cambodia. At the same time, more than 10 Cambodian divisions were deployed along Vietnam's border, with the troops under the command of Chinese advisers, Vietnam said.

An upsurge in the border skirmishes was reported Oct. 24 by the Vietnam news agency. It said thousands of Chinese troops and police and some Chinese planes had crossed the frontier in 19 separate incidents Oct. 13-17. Most of the raids were described as harrassing runs. These border clashes produced an acrimonious exchange of charges and counter-charges on the diplomatic level. The Vietnamese Foreign Ministry Nov. 2 issued a protest saying that "thousands of Chinese" had occupied strategic positions in Vietnam's Coalong province and had killed several Vietnamese soldiers when they opened fire. Peking rejected this protest. Hanoi radio also charged that China had dispatched at least 100,000 soldiers and advisers to Cambodia in further support of Pnompenh's fight against Vietnam.

A Chinese counterprotest lodged with Vietnam Nov. 7 accused Hanoi of having deliberately created "an extremely serious bloodshed incident along the Chinese-Vietnamese border area on Nov. 1." The note said six Chinese had died after being kidnapped. Peking also said that Chinese residing in the border area of Kwangsi Chuang Autonomous Region had been attacked by Vietnamese guards while removing Vietnamese roadblocks and filling in trenches that had been dug by the Vietnamese.

In an effort to assure themselves protection against possible Chinese attack, the Vietnamese turned to Moscow for an alliance. A high-level Vietnamese delegation headed by Communist Party Chairman Le Duan and Premier Pham Van Dong went to Moscow Nov. 2 to sign a 25-year treaty of friendship and cooperation. The signing of the treaty took place the following day, with President Leonid Brezhnev and Premier Alexei Kosygin representing the U.S.S.R.

The pact provided for "economic, scientific and technical cooperation with the purpose of accelerating socialist and communist construction." The Soviet Union specifically agreed to help improve strategic rail lines between Hanoi and the port of Haiphong and between Hanoi and Ho Chi Minh City (Saigon). The pact also pledged the signers, "in case one of the parties becomes the object of an attack, to begin mutual consultations immediately and take appropriate effective measures to insure the peace and security of their countries."

At a dinner after the signing ceremonies, Brezhnev declared that the treaty "holds special significance at this complicated moment when the policy of the Chinese leadership has created new, major difficulties for socialist construction on Vietnamese soil." This was an allusion to the border clashes between China and Vietnam, the latest one having occurred Nov. 1. Le Duan assailed China outright, asserting that it was "establishing a new alliance with imperialism and fascist hangers-on, an alliance against the socialist system and movement of national independence."

Peking reacted to the emergence of the new Moscow-Hanoi axis with a renewed attempt to solidify its relations with Southeast Asian countries. Chinese Communist Party Vice Chairman Wang Tung-sing led a high-level delegation to Pnompenh Nov. 5-6. Speaking at the banquet honoring the Chinese delegation, Wang reiterated China's support for the Cambodian people's "just struggle in defense of their independence." Pol Pot, Cambodian president, speaking at the same banquet, repeated the charge that Vietnam was planning a large-scale assault against his country in the dry season, due to start in December. He further charged that the Soviet Union "has enormously strengthened and enlarged its naval and missile bases in Vietnam."

Another Chinese delegation, led by Deputy Premier Teng
Hsiao-ping, visited Thailand, Malaysia, Singapore and Burma
Nov. 5-14 in a major diplomatic overture to those four anti-
communist Southeast Asian countries.

In a toast at a state dinner in Bangkok Nov. 6, Teng told his
Thai hosts that the Soviet Union posed "a serious threat to
world peace and security." He praised the Association of
Southeast Asian Nations, of which Thailand was a member,
saying it served to block the aims of Soviet "hegemonists."
Teng Nov. 8 assailed the Soviet-Vietnamese friendship treaty.
The pact was not "directed against China alone" but represented a threat to Asia and the world as a whole, Teng warned.
He said Vietnam had become the "Cuba of the Orient," suggesting that Hanoi was being used to promote the Soviet
influence in Asia.

After completing his tour of Thailand Nov. 9, Teng went to
Kuala Lumpur, Malaysia, where he sounded further warnings
to Vietnam. In a statement Nov. 10, he called on the Vietnamese to "draw back your criminal hand stretched to Chinese
territory and stop the provocation and intrusion" along the
frontier.

Vietnam Invades Cambodia

Fighting between Cambodia and Vietnam was stepped up in
late 1978 as the dry season approached. Vietnamese troops
made deep advances inside Cambodia the weekend of Nov.
18-19, and shattered, according to U.S. Administration sources, one Cambodian army division near the border of Snuol.
The Cambodian unit, estimated at 4,000 to 5,000 men, suffered
a "significant defeat with more serious losses than they have
taken" since the start of the frontier combat, the report said.

The Vietnamese push reached 10 miles (16 kilometers) north
of Snuol, heading in the direction of the strategic Mekong
River port of Kratie, the headquarters of Cambodia's eastern
administrative region, it was reported Dec. 6. Another column
of Hanoi's soldiers was advancing toward Kratie from the
Vietnamese-occupied border area of Mimot. The Vietnamese
troops pushed as far as 70 miles (112 kilometers) into southern

Cambodia, according to Western analysts in Hong Kong Dec. 14. This would put them in a position to sever Highway 4, linking Pnompenh to the main Cambodian port of Kompong Som on the Gulf of Siam.

Western diplomatic sources in Bangkok reported Dec. 21 that the thrust of Vietnamese troops into southern Cambodia appeared to have halted about 25 miles (40 kilometers) from Kratie. The sources expressed a belief that the advance had stopped about Dec. 11 but said they were not certain whether it was the result of Cambodian resistance or a deliberate Vietnamese decision to pause. Cambodia then reported Dec. 29 that the Vietnamese had launched a new drive Dec. 25 in the Mekong Valley north of Pnompenh but that its forces had repelled the assault, killing more than 1,000 Vietnamese.

Vietnam orchestrated its military operation with its political objective of overthrowing the Pol Pot regime. Hanoi radio announced Dec. 3 that a Kampuchean (Cambodian) United Front for National Salvation had been forced in Cambodia to attempt to unseat the Cambodian government. The announcement followed increased border fighting between Vietnam and Cambodia.

According to the Vietnamese broadcast, the front had been established in what it called a "liberated zone" of Cambodia, and the Vietnamese invaders had urged the Cambodian people "to rise up for the struggle to overthrow the Pol Pot-Ieng Sary clique." Without specifying where or when the new front had been created, the Hanoi broadcast said that more than 200 Cambodians from all walks of life had attended the founding conference. The meeting was said to have adopted an 11-point program of "tasks and goals." The conference had elected a 14-member central committee and named Hen Somrim as its leader, according to the Vietnamese. Hen Somrim was described by the broadcast as a former member of the "eastern region party organization" and political commissar and commander of an army division. The military arm of the new organization, Hanoi said, was called the Kampuchean Revolutionary Armed Forces.

A United Front statement broadcast by Hanoi radio Dec. 4 assailed the Cambodian government as "a dictatorial, milita-

rist and fascist regime, matchless in history for its ferocity."
The front echoed charges by Cambodian refugees of the
government's campaign of genocide against its own people,
asserting that Pol Pot and Ieng Sary had "totally usurped
power,... causing innumerable suffering and mourning to our
fellow Kampucheans and threatening our people with extermi-
nation." It accused the government of having "herded our
compatriots into camouflaged concentration camps, robbed
our people of all means of production and consumer goods,
... forcing all strata of the population to live in misery and
slavery." China, which supported Cambodia in its conflict with
Vietnam, was assailed by the United Front for having "encouraged and backed to the hilt these traitors and tyrants." The
statement accused the Pnompenh regime of having started the
war against Vietnam as a cover for its "abominable crimes
against our people." The United Front demanded the return of
all Cambodians who had been forced to flee the country and
promised that if it attained power it would create a planned
economy with markets, banks and currency, end forced labor
and establish an eight-hour work day with pay according to
work done.

Troops of Vietnam and the rebel Kampuchean United Front
for National Salvation were reported to have pushed closer
Jan. 4, 1979 to Pnompenh and Kompong Som, Cambodia's
only seaport, following an offensive they had launched inside
eastern Cambodia Dec. 25, 1978. Pnompenh condeded Jan. 4
that the Vietnamese and the rebels had captured one-quarter of
Cambodia and that Vietnamese troops and planes were attacking on eight fronts along the entire frontier between the two
countries. The insurgents Jan. 3 had claimed the capture of
three provincial capitals, putting them within 45 miles (72
kilometers) of Pnompenh. Western sources reported Jan. 4 the
capture of Takeo, just south of the Cambodian capital.

Pol Pot acknowledged Jan. 5 that his forces were engaged in
a "life-or-death struggle." He said "the army and the people ... are conducting a people's war against the hated Vietnamese invaders." The term "people's war" generally meant
guerrilla operations. In his first public statement since the start
of the drive, Pol Pot said "the struggle is continuing every-

where." Hostilities, he said, were raging in the three northeastern border provinces of Ratanakiri, Mondulkiri and Kratie, and to the south in Svay Rieng province and the adjacent area of Prey Veng, just east of Pnompenh. Pol Pot said that Vietnam was pressing its offensive with several divisions equipped with planes, tanks and artillery and that the drive had the support of the Soviet Union and other Warsaw Pact countries.

Rebels Form New Government

In an eleventh-hour measure to stay its impending doom, the Pol Pot government Jan. 2, 1979 brought an appeal to the United Nations Security Council. Cambodian President Khieu Samphan issued a statement Jan. 2 urging the U.N. and countries "far and near" to aid his country against the Vietnamese offensive, which, he claimed, was receiving the support of the Soviet Union.

The United States announced Jan. 3 that it would back Cambodia's bid for an emergency meeting of the U.N. Security Council, and it criticized Vietnam's role in the conflict. A State Department spokesman said that, while the Carter Administration "takes great exception to the human rights record" of Cambodia, as "a matter of principle, we do not feel that a unilateral intervention against that regime by a third power is justified." The Vietnamese offensive, the department stated, "involves intervention by armed force in the internal affairs of a sovereign nation." In a follow-up statement Jan. 4, the State Department said that while the U.S. supported Cambodia's request for a Security council meeting, it "does not prejudge the postion that we might take" in Council debate.

A spokesman for Vietnam's U.N. mission Jan. 4 called Cambodia's charges of Vietnamese aggression in requesting a Council meeting "flagrant calumnies." Cambodia was serving the expansionist policies of China and attempting to cover up serious military setbacks at the hands of the Cambodian rebel forces, the mission said.

Events outstripped the U.N. politics. In Cambodia, a combined force of Cambodian rebels and Vietnamese soldiers captured Pnompenh Jan. 7. The following day the insurgent

Kampuchean United Front for National Salvation formally announced the overthrow of the Pol Pot regime and its replacement by a People's Council of Cambodia. The Council, the announcement said, would be headed by Heng Samrin, the president. The other members of the Council were: Pin Sovan, vice president in charge of national defense; Hun Sen, foreign affairs; Chea Sim, interior; Keo Chanda, information, press and culture; Chan Ven, education; Nu Beng, health and social affairs, and Mok Sakun, economy and well-being of the people. Like Heng, all the Council members were believed to have defected from the Pol Pot government. Heng had first been identified in December 1978 with the announcement of the formation of the United Front. At the time, he was said to have been a former army division commander and political commissar in the Pol Pot government. A broadcast from Cambodia Dec. 5, 1978 had said that Heng had begun "revolutionary activities" in 1959, commanding first a battalion and then a regiment of the Cambodian Khmer Rouge forces. It said he led the Fourth Division and was its political commissar from 1976 until his defection in May 1978.

The new regime was on record as having pledged (in a broadcast Jan. 6) to abolish, in its "liberated zone," the excesses of the previous government, which had organized the entire nation into communes, separated families, emptied the towns and cities and destroyed the Buddhist religion and most of the country's traditional culture. The Front promised to reunite families and allow them to return to their former homes, restore freedom of religion and build and repair destroyed temples.

Fighting continued. Hanoi broadcasts attributed all military successes to the United Front without acknowledging the presence of Vietnamese troops in Cambodia. However, political, military and intelligence analysts in Bangkok, Thailand said the burden of battle was being carried by as many as 13 Vietnamese divisions and supporting troops, numbering about 100,000 men. While the United Front announced Jan. 8 that "Pnompenh and all the provinces of Cambodia were totally liberated," strong Cambodian government resistance was reported continuing in territory claimed captured by the Vietnamese, particularly east of the Mekong River near the Vietnamese border. By Jan. 12, Vietnamese columns were said to have advanced as far west as Battambang, near the Thai border, where heavy combat was in progress.

The Hanoi victory broadcast Jan. 7 also proclaimed the capture of Kompong Som, Cambodia's only seaport (on the Gulf of Siam) and the point of entry for almost all the military equipment China had sent to Cambodia. Cambodian government forces were reported Jan. 12 to be making their strongest stand in the west at Siem Reap, near the Angkor temple ruins. Heavy government resistance also was centered in the towns of Kompong Speu, Kompong Cham and Svay Rieng, to the south and east of Pnompenh, Bangkok intelligence sources reported.

The fall of Pnompenh produced long lines of refugees crossing into Thailand. Deputy Premier Ieng Sary was rescued by a Thai helicopter Jan. 11 and was flow to Bangkok. Denied Thai asylum, he flew to Hong Kong and crossed into China from there Jan. 12.

Premier Pol Pot was believed to have remained in Cambodia, diplomatic sources in Peking disclosed Jan. 10. Some members of the Chinese embassy in Pnompenh had also stayed in Cambodia and were thought to be with the premier, the sources said.

More than 700 foreign officials and advisers in Cambodia crossed into Thailand Jan. 8 to escape the Vietnamese drive. Among them was the Chinese ambassador to Cambodia. About 650 of the arrivals in the Thai border town of Aranyaprathet were Chinese, described by Thai officials as technicians, possibly military advisers. The other diplomatic corps escapees included North Koreans, Yugoslavs, Rumanians, Burmese and Egyptians.

In New York, the U.N. Security Council debated Jan. 11-12 the resolution formally introduced by China condemning the Vietnamese invasion of Cambodia. The debate was destined to be inconclusive, as the Soviet Union held a veto over the resolution. The United States and China both condemned the Vietnamese action, but the Soviet Union and other Warsaw pact countries except Rumania stood behind Vietnam. Developing countries in the non-aligned movement appeared uncertain and confused.

The most memorable development of the U.N. deliberation was the appearance of Cambodian Prince Norodom Sihanouk as the representative of the Pol Pot government. The prince had been kept under house arrest in Pnompenh since 1975 and been released only Jan. 5 for the purpose of attending the Security Council debate. At a six-hour press conference he gave at Peking on his way to New York, Sihanouk had confirmed accounts of atrocities in Cambodia under the Pol Pot regime. "I don't know why they chose to impose such a terrible policy on the people, but they told me it was a genuine communism," he said. Following the Security Council debate, Sihanouk was hospitalized in New York to recover from fatigue. Speaking with newsmen at the hospital Jan. 18, Sihanouk declared that he had no intention of returning to Cambodia. He had, he said, "already fulfilled my obligations" to the Pol Pot government and from now on he would speak out as a "free man, not as a representative" of the government. Sihanouk said he did not plan "to ask for asylum" in the U.S. But he reported that U.S. Secretary of State Cyrus Vance, who had visited him earlier in the day, "said I can stay here as long as I want to. And I do plan to stay here for awhile."

The civil war in Cambodia raged on. In a major counteroffensive, the Khmer Rouge, the forces of Pol Pot, recaptured at least part of the Gulf of Siam port of Kompot and also were said to have taken the Ream naval base, south of the major port of Kompong Som.

Despite the reported gains of the Khmer Rouge, the Vietnamese and their Cambodian insurgent allies were known to be in full control of the country. The rebel government in Pnompenh Jan. 20 insisted that its forces "totally controlled all the country's territory." It denounced "distorted foreign press reports" of the Pol Pot troop advances as the "propaganda trick of a number of big countries...who support Pol Pot in order to expand the war."

Kompong Som was recaptured by Khmer Rouge troops Jan. 15 but was taken back by Vietnamese forces, it was reported in Bangkok Jan. 18. Western sources in the Thai capital also said that several hundred Khmer Rouge soldiers, pursued by the Vietnamese, had crossed into Thailand Jan. 18 and were given asylum after being disarmed by Thai authorities. In fighting reported Jan. 19, Vietnamese troops attacked loyalist soldiers at the temple ruins of Preah Vihar on the Thai border, and Khmer Rouge troops recaptured the provincial capital of Takeo, which had been first seized by the Vietnamese invaders in their swift advance toward Pnompenh. The Khmer Rouge radio, thought to be broadcasting from Yunnan province in China, claimed Jan. 30 that Khmer Rouge forces had raided within 12 miles of Pnompenh.

China Invades Vietnam

Paralleling the developments in Cambodia, the tension along the Sino-Vietnamese border increased. Both sides were massing troops there. Vietnam was reported by U.S. intelligence officials Jan. 30, 1979 to have begun deploying troops along its border with China in the previous few days. Planes also had been brought to the Hanoi area to confront a possible Chinese air attack, according to the American report. The Vietnamese action, the Americans reasoned, was designed to counter a Chinese border buildup of at least 100,000 troops, several hundred tanks and about 150 planes.

China accused Vietnam Jan. 18 of having sent "armed personnel to encroach upon Chinese territory, open fire on Chinese personnel, killing and wounding, and looting Chinese fishing boats." Peking said four Chinese border guards were killed in incidents along 13 frontier regions between Dec. 23, 1978 and Jan. 15, 1979. The Chinese protest was in response to a Vietnamese note presented to the Chinese embassy in Hanoi Jan. 13. The Vietnamese message charged that between Jan. 8 and 12 Chinese forces had carried out nine border violations in which two persons were killed and three wounded. Hanoi charged Jan. 18 that Chinese troops had opened fire on a hill post in Vietnam's Cao Bang province and then occupied the post Jan. 15-16.

Carter Administration officials Jan. 21 expressed concern about the Chinese-Vietnamese frontier tensions. They were

said to fear that China, smarting over Hanoi's invasion of
Cambodia, Peking's principal ally, might invade Vietnam "to
teach the Vietnamese a lesson."

The war of words that accompanied clashes of arms continued well into February, pointing to an imminent outbreak
between China and Vietnam. This led the U.S. State Department to express its concern Feb. 9. A State Department statement said the Carter Administration hoped for "peace and a
stable system of independent states in Southeast Asia." The
U.S., it said, was "not taking sides in the struggle between two
Communist states in Asia." The department disclosed that the
U.S. had expressed its concern "directly to the Vietnamese,
Soviet and Chinese governments about the dangers of continued, perhaps expanded, fighting" in the region. The statement singled out China, saying, "We would be seriously
concerned over a Chinese attack on Vietnam." The U.S., the
statement added, also was troubled "over the continued Vietnamese attack" on Cambodia.

China received a similar warning from the Soviet Union
Feb. 8 against "overstepping the forbidden line" in Vietnam.
The Soviet journal *New Times*, expressing concern about the
reported Chinese buildup along the Vietnamese border, said
that since the Vietnamese had helped overthrow the Pol Pot
regime in Cambodia, the "snubbed dragon [China] wants to
show its claws" by moving against Hanoi.

The anticipated event occurred Feb. 17, 1979. About
200,000 to 300,000 Chinese troops backed by planes and
artillery struck along most of the 480-mile Sino-Vietnamese
frontier, with Vietnamese forces putting up stiff resistance. The
invading Chinese forces were under the command of a 73-year-
old general, Hsu Shih-yu, who was the head of the Canton
Military Region. The deputy commander of the operation was
Yang Teh-chih, head of the Kunming Military Region. Chang
Ting-fa, commander of the Chinese air force, was named chief
of staff.

The Chinese said they were retaliating for what they charged
were Vietnamese-instigated incidents along the Chinese border
and Vietnam's invasion of Cambodia. China's Hsinhua news
agency said Feb. 18 that China "did not want a single inch of
Vietnamese territory." It said that "after counterattacking the

Vietnamese aggressors as they deserve, the Chinese frontier troops will strictly keep to defending the border of their own country." In the past six months the Vietnamese had committed 700 armed attacks along the Chinese border and "killed or wounded more than 300 Chinese frontier guards and inhabitants," Hsinhua said. As a result, the Chinese news agency said, "the Chinese frontier troops are fully justified to rise in counterattack when they are driven beyond forbearance." China suggested that both sides meet to negotiate "the restoration of peace and tranquility along the border." Chinese Deputy Premier Teng Hsiao-ping was quoted Feb. 19 as describing his country's military operation as a limited "counterattack" and stating that it would not be "extended or expanded.... "

One official Vietnamese statement on the fighting came from Hanoi's ambassador to France, Vo Van Sung. He charged in Paris Feb. 19 that the Chinese invasion was "a veritable war of aggression" that had been "carefully prepared over several months." In view of Teng's visit to the U.S. Jan. 28-Feb. 1, China's attack had been "undertaken with the Americans' approval, if not their encouragement or collusion," Sung said.

As soon as the Chinese invasion started, Vietnam Feb. 17 appealed to the Soviet Union and "the fraternal socialist countries to support and defend Vietnam." Moscow did not respond immediately; the only mention of the conflict in the Soviet press was in a dispatch from Hanoi by Tass, the Soviet news agency, giving a brief description of the fighting.

The first official Soviet response, issued Feb. 18, warned China to "stop before it is too late." In blunt language the Soviet statement said, "All responsibility for the consequences of continuing the aggression... will be borne by the present Chinese leadership." The statement continued, "The heroic Vietnamese people... is capable of standing up for itself..., and furthermore it has reliable friends. The Soviet Union will honor its obligations under the Treaty of Friendship & Cooperation" that Moscow and Hanoi signed in 1978. Article VI of the treaty required the signatories "to begin mutual consultations" in the case of a threat to one of the signatories.

Moscow intensified its attack Feb. 19-20 to include charges that the U.S. was responsible for the Chinese invasion of Vietnam. A commentary Feb. 19 in *Izvestia*, the government newspaper, said U.S. and Western "'appeasers' of China [were] in a very ambiguous and politically vulnerable position." The statement was an allusion to the fact that China's attack had come soon after Teng's visit to the U.S. The Soviets went further Feb. 20, charging that the U.S. was directly responsible for the Chinese action. An article in *Pravda*, the Soviet Communist Party newspaper, said Teng had told U.S. officials during his visit that China had plans to invade Vietnam. *Pravda* said Teng was led to believe that the U.S. would take no action to prevent the attack. A statement the same day by Tass charged that "the war against socialist Vietnam was practically prepared by Peking with the tacit consent of Washington."

Contradicting the Soviet charges, the U.S. Feb. 17 called on China to withdraw its troops from Vietnam. At the same time, Washington criticized Vietnam for its invasion of Cambodia. A State Department spokesman said the U.S. was "opposed both to the Vietnamese invasion of Cambodia and the Chinese invasion of Vietnam." He continued, "The reported Chinese invasion of Vietnam, which we oppose, was preceded by the Vietnamese invasion of Kampuchea [Cambodia]," indicating that in Washington's view, the Vietnamese action was responsible for the Chinese invasion.

Despite China's earlier statements that its drive into Vietnam was limited, fighting intensified Feb. 20 after a reported short lull. Peking's troops continued their southward drive from the Lang Son area at the eastern end of their northern salient and from Lao Cai at the western end. Lang Son's 46,000 civilians were reported to have fled the town, but this report was considered unreliable.

In its initial account of the fighting, Vietnam reported Feb. 17 that Chinese forces that day had launched attacks on four border provinces from Quang Minh in the east to Hoang Lien Son in the west. (In its first report on casualties, Vietnam said Feb. 18 that its forces had killed hundreds of Chinese soldiers as they "checked" the Chinese advance six miles inside Vietnam. The report also said 60 Chinese tanks were knocked out. Vietnam Feb. 20 conceded the Chinese capture of Lao Cai, 175 miles northwest of Hanoi, on the railroad that ran from China's border province of Yunnan. At the same time, it claimed its forces had killed 5,000 Chinese since the start of the invasion. Hanoi added another 2,000 Chinese to the casualty toll Feb. 22. Western analysts regarded the Vietnamese figures as exaggerated and said they thought that the Vietnamese losses were heavier than the Chinese. China remained silent on the military developments.

Vietnam acknowledged Feb. 22 that the Chinese had pushed 15 miles inside the border area up to Cao Bang, 110 miles northwest of Hanoi. The Chinese, Hanoi said, were massing for an even "bigger attack." While Chinese planes were active, they were confined to the invasion areas, Vietnamese Deputy Foreign Minister Nguyen Thach said Feb. 22.

Moscow's military involvement was indicated in a report from Bangkok Feb. 22. The report said that the Soviet Union had begun airlifting military supplies to Vietnam. An earlier report Feb. 21 by Japanese military sources said the Soviet Union had sent four reconnaissance planes south past Japan to observe the fighting in Vietnam. The Soviets also were said to have reinforced their 11-ship fleet in the East China Sea, dispatching a cruiser and guided-missile destroyer. Most of the 11 ships were involved in intelligence gathering.

China warned the Soviet Union Feb. 21 against "armed intervention" in support of Vietnam. A communique issued by the Communist Party's Central Committee said China wanted "stable and peaceful borders" but would resist any Soviet attack.

Hanoi radio reported Feb. 26 that Chinese troops had advanced as far as 25 miles into Vietnam since the start of their invasion Feb. 17. Other sources placed the invaders at least 40 miles inside the country, having passed the captured provincial capital of Lao Cai. The Hanoi broadcast did not specify the region of the Chinese push, but Western sources in Bangkok said heavy fighting was continuing around Lang Son, in the eastern salient, about 85 miles northeast of Hanoi. The U.S. State Department said the combat was "heavier than before" and that "larger numbers" of soldiers of both sides were "apparently involved."

Chinese Deputy Premier Teng Hsiao-ping said Feb. 26 that he expected the fighting to end in "about 10 days or a few days more." Another Chinese official, Wang Chen, deputy premier for industry, had said Feb. 25 that his country had no intention of ordering its forces to drive beyond the present battle zone in the mountain region toward the populous Red River Delta or Hanoi.

Hanoi radio Feb. 26 denounced as a "deception" Peking's statements that it was carrying out a limited assault to retaliate for border violations. China, the Vietnamese said, was conducting a war of aggression "on a large and fierce scale." Vietnam continued to claim heavy losses inflicted on the Chinese. It said that in a three-day period that had ended Feb. 25, about 2,300 of the invaders had been killed or wounded, bringing their total losses since Feb. 17 to about 16,000. The Vietnamese continued to remain silent on their own casualties.

For the first time since the start of the invasion, China Feb. 27 reported the losses incurred by the Vietnamese. It said that between Feb. 17 and 26 Chinese troops had killed or wounded 17,000 Vietnamese and had captured 1,600 prisoners and brought them to China. The Chinese had destroyed seven Vietnamese missile sites near the border, according to the report.

President Carter called on China Feb. 27 to pull its troops out of Vietnam "as quickly as possible" because the invasion "ran risks that were unwarranted." The President's appeal was made in a personal message delivered by Treasury Secretary W. Michael Blumenthal to Deputy Premier Teng. Blumenthal had arrived in Peking Feb. 24 for negotiations to establish closer U.S.-Chinese economic relations.

At a meeting with American newsmen earlier Feb. 27, Teng likened Vietnam to Cuba, implying that both countries were involved in military adventures for the benefit of their ally, the Soviet Union. "Both the Cuba of the Orient [Vietnam] and the Cuba of the West seem to be emboldened by the so-called tremendous backing force behind them [the Soviet Union]," Teng said. The deputy premier added: "We cannot tolerate the Cubans to go swashbuckling unchecked in Africa, the Middle East and other areas, nor can we tolerate the Cubans of the Orient to go swashbuckling unchecked in Laos, Cambodia or even China's border areas." Asked about possible Soviet intervention on the side of Vietnam, Teng said Peking believed that the Soviets "will not take too big an action." In any event, he said, "we are prepared against them."

Peking indicated that it sought to end the invasion after a decisive battle that would "teach the Vietnamese a lesson." The site of the battle was Lang Son, the provincial capital, which the Chinese troops were reported to have captured March 1 after the heaviest fighting. Western analysts in Bangkok said the Vietnamese had finally abandoned the town or had been driven out. But Vietnam denied March 4 that Lang Son had been taken. Hanoi claimed that the Chinese advance had been checked a little more than a mile outside the town. The initial push launched by 72,000 Chinese troops five days earlier had been stopped by the defenders six miles outside Lang Son, according to the Vietnamese. By March 4, the fighting shifted to the outskirts of Lang Son and was so confused that neither side could claim its capture, Hanoi said.

According to China's version March 4 of the battle for Lang Son, the critical action came when Peking's troops seized a mountain north of the town. This promontory was described by the Hsinhua news agency as the "key position for launching attacks" against Lang Son. Soon after the capture of the heights, the Chinese force rushed forward and quickly took complete control of Lang Son, the Chinese report said.

Hanoi radio reported continued fighting around Lang Son March 5, claiming that "hundreds" of Chinese troops had been killed or wounded. The broadcast also told of 640 casualties inflicted on the Chinese in northwestern Hoang Lien Son province and said that a Chinese battalion had been "badly mauled" in Cao Bang province.

Chinese Troops Withdraw from Vietnam

The Chinese invasion of Vietnam ended as acrimoniously as it had started. An indication of China's intention to call a halt to the incursions had been expressed March 1 by Deputy Premier Li Hsien-nien. He said that Peking was "getting near" to achieving its aim of teaching the Vietnamese that its attacks along China's border would do no good. "Once our goal is achieved we will certainly withdraw our troops," Li said.

China and Vietnam exchanged proposals March 1 and 2 on the holding of negotiations. A note handed to the Vietnamese embassy in Peking March 1 expressed hope for "a settlement of the disputes between the two countries through peaceful negotiations." Vietnam rejected the Chinese suggestion March 2, charging that it was a ruse "to fool the public and cover up their war intensification." Hanoi instead proposed the holding of negotiations after the Chinese withdrew from Vietnam and Peking respected Vietnam's sovereignty and independence.

China announced March 5 that its forces were withdrawing from Vietnam after having "attained the goals set out for them" when they launched their invasion Feb. 17. Vietnam expressed doubts about Peking's intentions and charged that Chinese troops were continuing their attacks. The announcement by China's Hsinhua news agency, said that "starting March 5, all Chinese frontier troops are withdrawing to Chinese territory." Vietnam was warned that it "must make no more armed provocations and incursions along the Chinese border after the withdrawal of the Chinese frontier troops." China, the statement added, "reserves the right to strike back again in self-defense in case of a recurrence of such Vietnamese activities." Peking again appealed to Vietnam to meet with China "to discuss ways of insuring peace and tranquility along the border between the two countries and then proceed to settle the boundary and territorial disputes." Another Chinese statement March 6 on the pullout said Peking's troops were "victoriously returning" from Vietnam after having "exploded the myth of invincibility" of the Vietnamese army.

Three hours after China's March 5 withdrawal announcement, a Hanoi broadcast had said that Vietnam had ordered a "general country-wide mobilization." A decree of the National Assembly said "all citizens, of the age groups defined by law, shall join the armed forces according" to the government's plans. Despite China's withdrawal declaration, a Vietnamese army newspaper charged March 5 that Peking was "feverishly pouring more Chinese troops into Vietnam, stepping up its aggression, and its troops are frantically destroying Vietnamese villages." Vietnam made similar charges March 6 and 7. A Hanoi broadcast March 7 said Chinese troops "yesterday and this morning continued to carry out barbarous criminal acts, including plundering, bombing people's houses and wanton shellings." It specifically cited Chinese looting in villages around Lang Son and the shelling of Cao Bang and surrounding communities. The broadcast claimed that the Chinese were leaving Vietnam because they were "badly defeated," asserting that 45,000 of the invaders had been killed or wounded. To display its "goodwill for peace," Vietnam would not interfere with the Chinese pullout, but would strike back if the Chinese attacks continued, the Vietnamese Communist Party newspaper *Nhan Dan* said.

The Chinese announcement of withdrawal was received with skepticism in Moscow. Responding to the announcement, Moscow said March 5 that "there has been so far no information showing that China has actually been pulling its troops from Vietnamese territory." The Tass news agency accused China of sending more troops into Vietnam and threatening neighboring Laos. Tass said China's invasion had failed in its aim "to get us into a collision with the United States." The Soviet Union "can point out with legitimate pride" that it had not allowed itself to be provoked into a conflict with the U.S., Tass said.

Finally, March 15, China announced that its forces had completed their withdrawal from Vietnam.

Peking's announcement coincided with offers from Vietnam March 15 and 17 to hold talks to normalize relations between the two countries. A Vietnamese Foreign Ministry note broadcast over Hanoi radio March 15 acknowledged that the Chinese were leaving Vietnam but did not say the withdrawal was completed. The note repeated Vietnam's charges that the Chinese had destroyed bridges and buildings and looted villages as they pulled back. The ministry also said the Chinese had moved two border markers deep inside Vietnam from their original sites, reflecting Peking's intention permanently to occupy small parts of Vietnamese territory along the frontier. In its March 17 proposal, Vietnam said the holding of talks depended on the withdrawal of Chinese troops "still occupying many positions in Vietnamese territory."

Radio Hanoi March 19 again charged that Chinese troops were holding on to Vietnamese territory, despite Peking's claim that its forces had completed their withdrawal. Hanoi's charge was confirmed that day by Western military sources in Bangkok, who said an undetermined number of Chinese appeared to be deployed in strips of land more than one mile inside Vietnam.

China said May 2 that 20,000 of its men had been killed and wounded in the February-March war with Vietnam, while the Vietnamese had suffered 50,000 dead and wounded. China had a force of 200,000 men arrayed against 100,000 Vietnamese troops in the fighting, the report said. Vietnamese sources had informed U.S. reporters in Hanoi earlier in the week that 20,000 Chinese had been killed. (U.S. Defense Department officers speculated that on the basis of the usual ratio of one killed for every three wounded in combat, the Chinese fatality figures would total 5,000.)

Meanwhile, Hanoi charged May 9 that Chinese troops had crossed the border into Vietnam May 1-3 on sabotage missions and set fire to dozens of houses. The Chinese also had violated Vietnamese airspace over Lang Son province near the eastern end of the border, according to Hanoi.

Aftermath of the War

Chinese and Vietnamese representatives met in Hanoi April 18 and 26, 1979 in an attempt to restore normal relations disrupted by China's invasion of Vietnam. The two sides remained deadlocked after the two sessions. In the opening meeting April 18 Vietnamese Deputy Foreign Minister Phan Hien had offered the following three-point peace plan:

■ Both countries refrain from concentrating troops on their common border and withdraw all forces to about two or three miles from the frontier. A demilitarized zone be created in the vacated area.

■ Normal relations be established, with China and Vietnam refraining from the use or threat of force. Normal economic relations and transportation links be reestablished.

■ The border dispute and other territorial problems between the two countries be settled on the basis of agreements reached in 1887 and 1895 between the French colonial regime in Indochina and China. China and Vietnam exchange prisoners captured in their latest conflict.

In his address, Hien reiterated Hanoi's charge that Peking was solely responsible for the strife and rejected China's accusation that Vietnam had provoked the border incursions.

China rejected Vietnam's proposal at their second meeting April 26 and countered with a 10-point plan of its own. The plan, submitted by China's chief delegate, Deputy Foreign Minister Han Nian-long, demanded, among other things, that Vietnam withdraw its troops from Laos and Cambodia, that Hanoi pull out its small garrison from the Spratly Islands on the South China Sea and that it relinquish its claims to the Chinese-occupied Paracel Islands. Han also called on Vietnam to repatriate as many of the 200,000 ethnic Chinese who wanted to return and to stop mistreating those still in Vietnam. Han charged that Vietnam's proposal for a demilitarized zone "evades the crucial and substantive issues in the relations" between the two countries. He accused Vietnam of continuing "armed provocations" along the frontier.

Hien did not reply directly to the Chinese proposals but instead accused China of current violations of Vietnam's airspace and land and sea rights. He repeated charges that Chinese troops were occupying "over 10 points on Vietnamese territory" and that China still had a half million troops massed on the frontier.

Controlled Relaxation

Demonstrations for Democracy

The thaw in the internal policy of the People's Republic of China (PRC) was slow to unfreeze the skeptical attitude of the Chinese masses, who had been taught by their recent experiences to be wary of changes in political climate. The post-Mao leadership took pains to persuade the people that its new line in favor of democracy and human rights did not have a hidden agenda. Slow to respond at first, opposition surfaced in Peking and elsewhere in large Chinese cities through wall posters and street demonstrations. For a while, the new regime not only tolerated such an activity but seemed to encourage it. But there were inherent limitations to the liberalization policy, given the PRC's political structure and ideology. Trickles of dissent would not be allowed to turn into a torrent.

An impetus for more democracy and human rights derived also from the PRC's normalization of its diplomatic relations with the United States. As diplomats toasted the new relationship, crowds were forming in Peking demanding democracy, food and work. Demonstrators paraded the streets of the Chinese capital Jan. 8, 14 and 15, 1979.

The Jan. 8 rally, in which several thousand persons marched around Tien An Men Square, had been called ostensibly to commemorate the third anniversary of the death of Premier Chou En-lai. While others paid homage to Chou, the demonstrators carried banners that read: "We don't want hunger. We don't want to suffer any more. We want human rights and democracy." Political wall posters also appeared. One placard demanded the review of the case of three men from Canton who had been jailed for writing a wall poster in 1974 criticizing the Communist Party as a new elite class.

A group of 100 to 200 peasants from various parts of China arrived in Peking Jan. 14 in an unsuccessful effort to present their grievances to government officials. Police barred them from seeing Deputy Premier Teng Hsiao-ping or Communist Party Chairman Hua Kuo-feng. The peasants carried banners with the slogans: "Persecuted people from all over China," "We want democracy and human rights," and "A plea for help from Teng Hsiao-ping." Many of the marchers shouted,

"We're tired of being hungry" and "Down with oppression."
The demonstrators drew a crowd of about 1,000 onlookers.
They quietly ended their protests Jan. 15. Similar demonstrations errupted in Shanghai a little later. The official news
agency Hsinhua Feb. 10 quoted a Shanghai official as saying
that since the end of January "there has been a small group of
young people blocking traffic, damaging public property...,
assailing cadres and stopping moving trains."

Foreign visitors to Shanghai were reported to have seen
protests by thousands of young people who had been resettled
in the countryside under the Cultural Revolution's "Youth to
Countryside" program, which was being phased out. The
young people had denounced their assignments and poor living
conditions. Many of the demonstrators either had left the rural
villages to which they were sent and drifted back to the city or
had complained that the factories to which they had been
assigned after finishing their terms on farms were too far from
their homes in Shanghai, it was reported.

Prompted by such disturbances, the Chinese government
issued warnings. The CCP (Chinese Communist Party) newspaper *Jenmin Jih Pao* said Feb. 12 that while some people had
legitimate grievances, they should "bear in mind the country's
overall interests and work wholeheartedly for modernization."
Demonstrators "deliberately creating trouble that has serious
consequences" would be punished the newspaper said.

Deputy Premier Teng Hsiao-ping, in a speech delivered to
Communist Party officials March 16, warned Chinese citizens
against pushing for democratic reforms. He said that some had
revealed sensitive information to foreigners, indicating that
they had passed along secrets in dancing with foreigners or
visting foreign embassies in Peking. Teng also denounced Chinese who complained about alleged violations of human rights
in posters and in letters sent to U.S. President Jimmy Carter
and U.S. Ambassador Leonard Woodcock. The deputy premier referred to the case of one of the protesters, a woman
linked with the movement for freer expression in China, who
had been arrested on undisclosed charges. Teng was said to
have called for an open trial for her. Teng said that China's war
with Vietnam was delaying his government's dealing with political liberalization and other problems.

The essence of Teng's speech was repeated in an editorial published March 18 in *Jenmin Jih Pao*, which assailed "the dirty work of certain traitors who sell national secrets and harm the national interest." The editorial warned that the government would "not deal gently" with the human rights activists, saying they would be arrested and tried if they continued their protests. The newspaper complained that demonstrators "waving the signboards of democracy" had created public disturbances, stormed government offices, beat people and sabotaged "normal order in work, production and society."

Following up on these warnings, the Chinese authorities began a crackdown against protestors April 1, ordering workers to remove posters from walls in the center of Peking. The decision to take down the placards and prohibit any rally or publication regarded as anti-government and anti-Communist had been made by the Peking City Revolutionary Committee March 29. The committee's action, announced March 31, could subject violators of the rules to "physical labor, education and discipline." Peking residents were not permitted to "put up or write slogans, advertising posters, . . . at public places and on buildings except at designated places." The authorities also placed a ban on slogans, posters, books, periodicals and photographs opposed to "socialism, against the proletarian dictatorship, against the leadership of the Communist Party, against Marxism-Leninism and Mao Tse-tung thoughts."

The government's restrictions were denounced by activists in a mimeographed statement circulated in Peking April 1. The document, called *Exploration*, said the decision "only demonstrates to the whole world that the Chinese government does not want any true democratic freedoms. The so-called true democracy and freedom which they talk about is only an order to the Chinese people to bolster the prestige of the authorities which are in power."

Moving Closer to the West

Undeterred by Peking's curbs on human rights, the normalization of relations with the United States proceeded on course. The post-Mao leadership envisaged the "four modernizations" to be pursued in close association with the Western Europe, Japan and the United States. It looked to the West for industrial technology, capital and markets for China's export goods, which sharply contrasted with the Maoist emphasis on self-reliance. The overriding importance attached by Peking to its modernization goals took ideology out of its foreign policy orientations. While it moved closer to the West, its relations with the Soviet Union continued to deteriorate.

Finally, Peking informed the Soviet Union April 3 that it had decided not to extend its 1950 friendship treaty with the Soviet Union when it expired in 1980. The decision had been taken by the Standing Committee of the National People's Congress (the legislature) April 2. The Hsinhua news agency said that "great changes had taken place in the international situation and the treaty had long ceased to exist except in name owing to the violations for which the Chinese side is not responsible."

The Soviet Union April 4 denounced China's decision to permit the pact to lapse. Peking's action, a Soviet government statement said, "was taken contrary to the will and interests of the Chinese people.... All responsibility for the termination of the treaty rests with the Chinese side."

Moscow indicated, however, that it was willing to open talks with Peking on border disputes and other conflicts. Peking did not reject the Soviet request out of hand, which led to speculation that the Chinese government might moderate its harsh stand against the Soviet Union. The *Washignton Post* reported May 29 that this caused a serious split within the Chinese leadership. A broadcast from the southeastern part of Hunan province openly criticized Teng Hsiao-ping on this and on other matters dealing with his agricultural policy and his handling of domestic dissent. The Hunan broadcast warned that China should not "beg" for a change in relations but should rely on the "strong power of the proletariat." In May, the *Post* reported, Hunan radio had broadcast a tribute to the village of Tachai, an agricultural collective often praised by Mao. Teng's supporters had recently criticized Tachai for preventing its peasants from cultivating private plots and for ignoring individual initiative. Sinologists noted that it was the first public praise for Tachai in several weeks.

Meanwhile, Teng and his supporters had begun a campaign to respond to the criticism. Press articles called for unity with the current party policy and criticized Teng's opponents for relying completely on Mao. The pro-Teng articles refuted claims that Teng's call for democracy had resulted in protest wall posters and unrest. "Of course, some places have gone a bit astray in various ways," said a broadcast cited May 25 by the *New York Times*. "However, the emergence of these problems is certainly not caused by the party's policies themselves, but by variations in their execution." Teng himself replied to his critics, according to a report released by the Taiwan intelligence agency. In a speech thought to have been made in March, Teng said, "We should let people put up posters. . . . We will be able to avoid making the masses angry."

In the meantime, the PRC's foreign economic relations expanded rapidly. An agreement was signed in Paris May 9 to permit China to borrow $7 billion from a group of 18 French banks through 1985. It was believed to be the largest loan ever negotiated by China. The accord was negotiated within the framework of a trade agreement signed by France and China in December 1978. The money to be obtained from the French banks would be used to finance Peking's purchases of French industrial goods and services, possibly including two nuclear power stations. The credit line included inexpensive French government funds provided by the government-controlled Francaise Banque du Commerce Exterieur, with interest rates varying between 7.25% and 7.50%. The bank's head, Francoise Giscard d'Estaing, said China was unlikely to make much immediate use of the new credit facility. He said this was because "it takes time" to build the needed accompanying facilities for major projects, such as an aluminum factory.

The conclusion of the French loan agreement was followed by the initialing of a trade pact with the United States May 14. The trade agreement would set up formal commercial relations between China and the United States for the first time since the establishment of the PRC in 1949. Chinese Foreign Trade Minister Li Chiang initialed the pact in Peking, and U.S. Commerce Secretary Juanita Kreps initialed the document in Canton. The agreement required approval by the two governments, as well as the U.S. Congress, before taking effect. The pact would lower tariff restrictions on most Chinese exports to the U.S. by granting Peking most-favored-nation trading status. An agreement on the amount of Chinese textile exports to the U.S., however, remained to be worked out. Vice Foreign Trade Minister Chen Chieh complained that the quotas demanded by the U.S. remained too low. (In 1978, the U.S. exported $824 million worth of goods to China and imported $324 million worth of Chinese goods.)

The major obstacle to the U.S. trade agreement had been overcome when Kreps and Chinese negotiators signed an accord in Peking May 11 on mutual public and private financial claims. The agreement was the same as a draft initialed in Peking March 1 by Chinese officials and U.S. Treasury Secretary W. Michael Blumenthal. It provided for China to settle American claims by a payment of $80.5 million, of which $30 million was to be paid Oct. 1 and the remainder in five annual installments of $10.1 million starting Oct. 1, 1980. The payments were to be distributed to claimants by the U.S. government. The U.S. in turn would unblock $80.5 million in Chinese-related assets by Oct. 1.

In addition to the trade and claims agreements, the United States and China May 8 had approved exchanges in scientific, technological and business affairs. The following accords had been announced by Kreps May 13:

■ The two countries would cooperate in such scientific and technological areas as precision measurements and standards, building technology, analytical chemistry, materials research and applied mathematics.

■ China and the United States would exchange scientific and technological reports, establish joint conferences and exchange experts in the scientific and technical managements field.

■ Oceanographers and fishery scientists of the two countries would trade information under a marine agreement.

■ An agreement provided for exchanges of trade exhibitions by U.S. and Chinese businessmen.

■ A meterological accord would establish cooperation in atmospheric science and technology.

U.S. Congressional approval was believed contingent on a textile agreement. Congress was under strong pressure from

U.S. textile manufacturers who wanted their industry protected from stiff Chinese competition. A month-long negotiation in Peking in May failed to break the impasse. Forward the end of the month President Carter sent his special trade representative Robert S. Strauss to Peking in an effort to expedite the talks. Strauss arrived in the Chinese capital May 26. He met with Deputy Premier Teng Hsiao-ping May 30 and conferred with other Chinese officials May 31. The impasse was not broken in spite of these high-level talks. A report from Peking June 1 attributed the breakdown in the textile talks to the U.S. "Despite efforts and concessions by the Chinese side, the American side adhered to its proposed limited quotas," the Chinese news agency Hsinhua said. The negotiations had been conducted under what was known as the Multi-Fiber Agreement, an arrangement signed in Geneva to limit the growth of textile imports from 18 developing nations. Strauss said May 31 that the issue discussed was "part of a common problem we both seek to solve." He referred to China's need to earn foreign currency for import of foreign technology from the United States and other industrialized nations. Peking sought to use revenues from its textile exports as a major source of foreign currency.

The United States May 31 imposed quotas on five categories of textile imports from China: cotton work gloves, cotton blouses, cotton shirts, cotton trousers and synthetic fiber sweaters. The imports in these categories were to be limited over the following 12 months to levels existing in the 12 months ended Feb. 28. The imposition of the quotas left the door open to future negotiations, however.

The formal signing of the treaty took place in Peking July 7, with Foreign Trade Minister Li Chiang representing China and Ambassador Leonard Woodcock signing for the United States. To take effect, the pact still required approval by the U.S. House and Senate. The new tariffs set by the pact would lower the average impost on Chinese goods to 5.7 per cent of their value from the current average of about 34 per cent. Other provisions allowed U.S. companies to set up business offices in China and afforded patent, trademark and copyright protection. The Commerce Department estimated that the agreement, if approved by Congress, could lead to a doubling in

1979 of the $1.1 billion in two-way trade registered in 1978. Annual two-way trade could reach $5 billion in five years, the department predicted.

The new trade accord gave China most-favored-nation tariff treatment. The formal signing of the agreement was delayed because the Carter Administration was reportedly trying to reach a similar agreement with the U.S.S.R.—in keeping with its policy to deal even-handedly with the Soviet Union and China. U.S. law barred extending most-favored-nation status to countries that did not permit free emigration. Progress on the Soviet treaty had been blocked by a refusal of the Soviets to give assurances on the emigration question, but Chinese officials reportedly had said they did not object to free emigration. A U.S. official was quoted July 4 as saying that "the China agreement is going forward because it's ready, and there is no reason to penalize the Chinese because of the Russians."

Anticipating increases in foreign investment in China, Peking July 8 announced a code covering foreign companies that invested in joint-venture enterprises in China. The law left some matters vague or unstated—including the level of corporate and individual tax rates—but it also provided certain guarantees and incentives designed to attract foreign investors. In particular, the code promised that foreign companies and their employees would be permitted to remit abroad after-tax earnings in foreign currencies. It also said that companies that brought "up-to-date technology by world standards" to China would get a full or partial exemption from taxes for the first two or three years they made a profit.

Although the code did not specify the maximum share of an enterprise that could be held by foreign investors, Chinese officials had indicated that in most cases foreign ownership would be limited to 49 per cent, it was reported July 9. However, 100 per cent ownership would be permitted in some cases, and the law stipulated that the foreign share had to be at least 25 per cent. The code said that the chairman of each joint-venture company would be appointed by the Chinese, but other high-level executives could be appointed by the foreign partner. Hiring and firing procedures would be "stipulated according to law in the agreement or contract concluded between the parties to the venture," the code said.

Other provisions of the joint-venture law included the following:

■ Foreign partners who reinvested earnings in China would qualify for rebates of taxes already paid.

■ The joint ventures could sell their products in China or abroad, using Chinese export corporations or their own facilities.

■ Arbitration would be used to settle disputes.

■ The ventures would be permitted to borrow funds directly from foreign banks.

The Chinese news agency Hsinhua said that two new offices were being created to deal with joint-venture proposals. One, the Foreign Investment Control Commission, would decide whether to approve specific proposals; the other, the China International Trust Investment Co., would "coordinate the use of foreign investment and technology."

Vice President Mondale Visits Peking

The rapidly developing U.S.-Chinese rapprochement received its symbolic recognition through an official visit of U.S. Vice President Walter Mondale to Peking. Mondale arrived in the Chinese capital Aug. 25, 1979 for a week-long visit. He held talks with Deputy Premier Teng Hsiao-ping and Chairman Hua Kuo-feng Aug. 27-28. At a banquet given in Mondale's honor Aug. 26, Teng warned that "the danger of war is still growing" and urged that the United States and China oppose "hegemonism," Peking's phrase for Soviet expansion. Mondale replied that the U.S. also opposed "efforts by any country to dominate another" and expressed hope that "the Sino-American relations can emerge in the 1980s as one of the major bulwarks of peace and justice in the world."

After their meetings Aug. 28, Mondale, Teng and Hua signed an expanded cultural exchange pact and a protocol under which the U.S. would help China develop hydroelectric power. Under the latter agreement, experts of the U.S. Army Corps of Engineers, the Tennessee Valley Authority, the Department of Energy and the Bureau of Reclamation would help China plan, design and supervise construction of 20 projected power-generating dams. The cultural accord put into effect a generalized agreement signed by Teng and President Carter in Washington Jan. 31. This included the exchange of visits of English and Chinese language experts, of staffs of Voice of America and Radio Peking and of books and of documents of the Peking Library and the Library of Congress.

In reporting on his two days of talks, Mondale said at a news conference Aug. 28 that his meetings with Teng and Hua were "extremely productive and friendly" and helped move the normalization of relations between China and the U.S. into "concrete reality." The friendship between the two countries "is not directed against anyone," and the United States did not "anticipate a military relationship" with China, Mondale asserted. Mondale said that his discussions with Teng and Hua also dealt with Indochina, Taiwan, Korea and the strategic arms treaty between the U.S. and the Soviet Union. He said he had agreed with both Chinese leaders that the "puppet government" installed by Vietnam in Cambodia was "insupportable." Also discussed was a political solution to the Cambodian problem that involved neither Heng Samrin, the Vietnamese-supported leader, nor former Premier Pol Pot, who had China's support, Mondale said. Mondale said Hua had accepted President Carter's invitation to visit the United States sometime in 1980 and that Carter would visit China.

In a televised speech from Peking University Aug. 27, Mondale had declared that a "strong and modernizing" China was in the interest of the United States. "Despite the sometimes profound differences between our two systems, we are committed to joining you to advance our many parallel and bilateral interests," the vice president said. He cautioned that "any nation which seeks to weaken or isolate you in world affairs assumes a stance counter to American interests," an apparent reference to the Soviet Union. Mondale also disclosed that the United States was prepared to lend China $2 billion over a five-year period through Export-Import Bank credits. "If the pace of development warrants it, we are prepared to consider additional credit agreements," Mondale said.

At a briefing later with Western reporters, U.S. officials said that Mondale's promise of quick congressional action on the U.S.-Chinese trade agreement signed in May and his warnings against isolation of China did not mean any "tilting" of American policy toward China. "It remains the policy of the United States to seek improved relations with both China and the Soviet Union," the officials said.

Economic Difficulties

While economic relations with the West were being opened, the PRC in the spring of 1979 was experiencing considerable economic difficulties.

A Hong Kong newspaper July 14 reported confirmation of this situation in a speech attributed to Vice Premier Li Hsien-nien. Speaking before a Peking conference in April, Li detailed serious economic problems facing the country, including unemployment and malnutrition. Twenty million Chinese, Li was reported as having said, were unemployed, and 100 million people did not have enough to eat. He added that the government faced a budget deficit of $6 billion. Li indicated that Peking would have to cut back on government spending and channel money into agricultural production instead of industrial development. "China has a poor economic base," Li was reported as saying. "The sabotage done to the state's economy by the 'Gang of Four' cannot be repaired in a short time."

The government deficit reportedly resulted from compensation paid to purged officials who were rehabilitated as well as from too-rapid industrial development. It was also said to have grown out of a 1977 pay increase for industrial and clerical workers and a series of bonuses for higher productivity.

Another indication of economic difficulties surfaced when Chinese Foreign Trade Minister Li Chiang May 6 announced that China was cutting back on its ambitious economic development program, a move that involved retrenchment in heavy-industry imports of capital goods in the immediate future. Despite the change, Li said, China was not abandoning its campaign of "Four Modernizations"—in agriculture, industry, science and technology, and defense. Nor did it wish to end cooperation with the United States to achieve those goals, he said. According to Li's explanation of the new policy shift: "The readjustment of our economy undertaken at this moment is exactly for the purpose of concentrating our efforts in the most needed projects and quickening the pace for the Four Modernizations." Li made his statement in a toast to U.S. Commerce Secretary Juanita Kreps, who had arrived in Peking May 5 for a two-week visit to help restore normal trade relations between the U.S. and China.

Premier and Communist Party leader Hua Kuo-feng acknowledged June 18 that China's economic goals for 1979 had been too ambitious. Hua said China would have to cut back on some of the development plans adopted in 1978. In a speech to the opening session of the National People's Congress, China's nominal legislature, Hua admitted that "some of the measures we adopted [in 1978] were not prudent enough." He said three years would be required before China could embark on a program of high-speed economic development. Hua told the 3,300 delegates that expansion of light industries would proceed more quickly in 1979 than developmenmt of heavy industry. He promised more consumer goods, increased salaries and increased exports.

For the first time since the 1950s, the Chinese regime provided figures on China's past economic performance. Hua said grain output for 1978 was 304.75 million metric tons, a 7.8 per cent increase over 1977. (A metric ton is 2,204.6 pounds.) Total industrial output, Hua continued, had increased 14 per cent in 1978 over the year before. He said steel output had totaled 31.8 million metric tons, coal output 618 million metric tons and crude oil 104 million metric tons in 1978.

Steadying the Course

The return to pragmatic management of the Chinese state and society according to bureaucratic criteria created its own problem: the emergence of a bureaucratic elite separate from the masses. It was the very spectre that Chairman Mao had tried to exorcise through the Cultural Revolution.

About 1,000 Chinese attended a rally in Peking's Tien An Men Square Sept. 13, 1979 in a demonstration denouncing special privileges among Communist Party officials and urging more human rights and free elections. The gathering was sponsored by a group calling itself the Democratic Scientific & Socialist Study Association. One of the speakers asserted that the principal problem in China "is the contradiction between the powerful privileged class and the workers. We have wiped out capitalists, landlords and rich peasants, but now we have a new rich class." Another speaker said he had not been connected with the society but decided to address the rally after learning that its leaders had disappeared Sept. 12, apparently arrested. He declared that "human rights is not a capitalist term, it has no class nature." He assailed "bureaucrats" who enjoyed all the privileges of their class "while many people's stomachs are empty."

In previous dissident actions in Peking, high school graduates Sept. 10 staged a protest march to the city's government offices, charging they had been refused admission to college after passing their entrance examinations. On Sept. 9 a group of 300 writers met in a park to discuss the state of official and underground literature. Another demonstration of Chinese protesting their poor economic condition was held outside government offices Sept. 6. They attached a poster outside the building promising not to leave "until we are victorious." The demonstrators, all of whom were unemployed and poor, were seeking redress for a variety of grievances, many of them dating to the Cultural Revolution of the 1960s. Demonstrations by protesters varying in number continued off and on through the month.

The Chinese government responded to the mounting unrest by promising speedy measures for investigation. The official Chinese Communist Party newspaper *Jenmin Jih Pao* reported Sept. 15 that the government had set up a special commission of 1,000 officials to look into the complaints of the petitioners, estimated to number as many as 20,000. The officials would hear the petitioners' cases and then escort the petitioners back to their native areas, where local officials would resolve the problems. The government acknowledged that "in some areas and units, a few wrong and false cases have not yet been resolved" and "some petitioners have been retaliated against after returning to their native places." The paper continued, "70 to 80 percent of the petitioners have come to Peking repeatedly."

Meanwhile, rehabilitation of the victims of the Cultural Revolution continued. The CCP Central Committee announced Sept. 28 that it had added to its membership 12 persons, all of whom had been victims of the Cultural Revolution. One of the 12, Peng Chen, was named also to the party's ruling Politburo. Peng had been mayor of Peking before he was ousted during the Cultural Revolution. Also promoted to the Politburo was Chao Tsi-yang, the party first secretary of Szechwan province.

In a speech Sept. 29 commemorating the 30th anniversary of the People's Republic of China, Communist Party Senior Deputy Chairman Yeh Chien-ying described the Cultural Revolution of the late 1960s as "an appalling catastrophe suffered by all our people." Yeh listed a number of errors the Communist Party had made in the late 1950s and the 1960s, and emphasized that China must now "seek truth from facts," or in other words adopt a pragmatic, nondogmatic approach to matters. The late Communist Party Chairman Mao Tse-tung was described as a great man whose leadership was vital to the success of the revolution before 1949. But, Yeh added, Mao was not a god. Mao's thought, Yeh said, was "not the product of Mao Tse-tung's personal wisdom alone. It is also the product of the wisdom of his comrades in arms."

Although the late head of state Liu Shao-chi was not named by Yeh, his speech appeared to approve of Liu's actions and take a step toward Liu's posthumous rehabilitation. Liu had been purged in 1968 during the Cultural Revolution. Yeh said the Eighth Party Congress, which took place in 1956 and at which Liu had presented the political report, had been completely correct. That meeting had been denounced at the next party congress, which was held in 1969 during the Cultural Revolution. Yeh said that the campaign against right-wingers, which followed the short-lived Hundred Flowers period of political liberalization in 1957, had gone too far. Of the Great Leap Forward in 1958, Yeh said, "We made mistakes in giving arbitrary directions, being boastful and stirring up a communist wind." Liu had opposed Mao on that movement.

Important steps undoubtedly were taken to bring some democratic freedoms to the People's Republic of China, but the events of 1979 and early 1980 provided reason to conclude that the road to full democracy in the PRC was likely to be a long and tortuous one—and possibly might be a path with no end.

Index

199